# RISING
# STAR

## ACHIEVING YOUR FULL POTENTIAL
## IN SPORTS AND LIFE

### DAVID HILL AND DAN VALAHU, Ph.D.

© 2016 David Hill and Dan Valahu
First edition
Published by David Hill and Dan Valahu
Waco, Texas

11 12 13 14 15 16 17 18 19 20—10 9 8 7 6 5 4 3 2 1

ISBN: 978-1537105550

Book design by Paraclete Press
Front cover design by John Howard

Library of Congress Cataloging-in-Publication Data


PRINTED IN THE UNITED STATES OF AMERICA

The paper used in this publication meets the minimum requirements of the American National Standard for Information Sciences—Permanence of Paper for Printed Library Materials, ANSI Z39.48-1992.

To my wife Laura. To my children Chris, Lacy, Holly, Lauren, and grandchildren.

**—DAVID HILL**

In memory of Pascal and Ana. To Claude, Carolyn, and Diane.

**—DAN VALAHU**

# Contents

## PART III:
# THE PSYCHOLOGY OF THE ELITE ATHLETE

## PART IV:
# PERSONAL BEHAVIOR AND TEAMMATE RELATIONSHIPS

# Introduction

---

*To follow the path,*

*look to the master,*

*follow the master,*

*walk with the master,*

*see through the master,*

*become the master.*

—Zen proverb quoted by Jim Afremow

**IN 2003 I (DAVID HILL) WAS INDUCTED**
into the International Martial Arts Hall of Fame as Hapkido and Tae Kwon Do Instructor of the Year. I was considered to be one of the best mixed martial artists and trainers of my era. At the same time, being a champion and knowing a good number of champions in varied athletic fields made me realize that I was not always the hardest worker or the most knowledgeable. Neither was I the fastest or strongest. What I did possess in abundance, and still do, was the ability to control my thoughts and emotions under the most adverse conditions. The athletes who control their minds and emotions are the individuals who reach world champion status the most consistently. They are the ones who use mind control and self-discipline to maintain a superior work ethic which, in turn, produces superior competitive results.

Michael Jordan, Larry Bird, Mia Hamm, Muhammad Ali, Wayne Gretzky, Michael Phelps, and Lindsey Vonn, among many others, all believed they were the best due to long-standing psychological convictions. These athletes believed in themselves, were never burdened by strong doubts even when they struggled in their sport. They possessed a burning desire to be the best in their respective fields. Above all, they consistently pushed themselves to maintain a high-caliber work ethic in adverse as well as ideal conditions. Despite the normal setbacks early in their careers, they were nonetheless convinced they would ultimately prevail.

Parallel to training outstanding athletes, I have worked with many Special Forces military soldiers and Secret Service men and women. The main thing I teach them is how to control their minds (to neutralize thoughts that lead to emotions such as fear and anger) so that they are prepared in a focused, quick-to-react adroitness in worst-case scenarios. I have also worked with them to ensure a consistent, high-caliber work ethic.

Early on when I was training amateur and professional client-athletes, I realized that I was not stressing mind control enough. That is when I started helping them to write self-talk (auto-suggestive) scripts and showing them how to visualize, or vividly imagine a pre-enactment of a desired sport-related skill. I urged them to make audio recordings related to their ambitions, then to listen to these recordings in their free time or on their way to a competition and, most beneficially, before going to bed and upon rising. I taught them how to role play (auto-suggestive vivid imagining of themselves functioning physically, in preparation for a competitive event) and to control their body language on the court or field so that they would always look confident. I have been able to achieve great results with my clients.

And I can teach you, too. If you picked up this book, it's likely because you possess a strong desire to become an elite athlete or to reach your full athletic potential. Dan and I understand. You are the reason we wrote this book. Follow the "prescriptions" contained herein and you will become the athlete you dream of being.

Prepare yourself for the adventure of your life. Prepare yourself to learn and to practice mind-control—that is, self-talk, auto-suggestion, and visualization. Prepare yourself to find out who you really are: simply a better-than-average human being who sometimes compromises or an exceptional one.

Read the following chapters with care, for there is much to absorb and new values to cherish. Based on your unique interpretation of our suggestions, the personal blueprint to greatness you choose will not be easy to follow. Gone will be the days when you regularly retire late at night and rise at a late morning hour. Your training regimen will no longer be arbitrary, based on how you feel on a given day. And when you celebrate victory—which will be more and more often—you won't do so by eating a pizza and consuming a beer or soft drinks.

By reading this book and mastering its strategies, you will benefit from and enjoy the same success that my client-athletes and I have achieved. Beyond the ultra-essential tools, this book will travel into many other significant areas to ensure that you take full advantage of the extant cutting-edge approaches to training, eating, hydrating, visualizing, and performing at the highest level. Moreover, this volume covers areas such as coaching, sports injuries and their prevention, goal-setting, preparation for workouts, and many more positive strategies that we feel are crucial in your development.

Embarking on the training of the body, particularly in the off-season, without first beginning to train the mind is counter-productive. The ambitious athlete seeking improvement, as well as the athlete pursuing elite status, must recognize that the brain functions much as a muscle: the more it is trained through self-talk, auto-suggestion, and visualization, the stronger it becomes. Consequently, the mind prepares the body to perform at its optimum capacity in a focused, fearless, and determined manner. That's why Part I of this book focuses on mastering your mind and emotions—it's the foundation for all the other topics we'll cover in the later chapters, like developing a work ethic, setting goals, being coachable, and dealing with failure—and success.

Well, what say you? Are you on board? Take this book. Treat it like your Bible. Once you've decided on your tailor-made workout plan, do not waver from it, unless the training experience dictates needed adjustments. As you follow your master plan, we are convinced that your mind, heart, and soul will burn with one overriding idea: *I will astound my coaches and teammates on the first day of pre-season practice or training. As they observe me, I will display explosively fluid power, speed, and agility. As the first practice nears its end, I will demonstrate a newfound endurance. I will carry out my coaches' instructions and gain a new appreciation of their ways and principles. Essentially, in everyone's eyes, I will have attained a highly improved level of performance or, even, elite athletic status. Above all, I will enjoy my new identity.*

So, read, absorb, apply, and transform yourself into the athlete you always dreamed of becoming.

# PART 1

# MIND CONTROL

# 1
# Controlling Your Mind and Emotions

———

*One of the best ways of learning self-control is to talk to yourself. . . . It*
*works. When faced with difficult decisions or a crisis, sit down and act*
*it out in your mind, if necessary actually do so out loud. . . .*
*By acting out in advance, we do more than simply rehearse a situation.*
*We prepare ourselves for it, we reduce anxiety . . . and we increase our*
*capacity for calm self-control.*

—Michael Korda

**IN ORDER TO TRAIN AND PERFORM**
at your best, it is essential to learn to control your mind and emotions in a
consistent manner. Successfully completing a rigorous workout schedule is only
one element in a multi-faceted program to make you the best that you can be.
To be an elite or outstanding athlete, you must be able to control your thoughts
and feelings. This mastery is so important that we won't cover some of the other
topics in this book—things like physical training, nutrition, and coaching—until
we've addressed it.

The mind is powerful. Whatever you tell yourself over and over, your mind
and your unconscious will store and believe. Moreover, mind control will enable
you to consistently manage your eating and drinking habits and push your body
through strenuous workouts. With mind control, you will be able to govern

powerful emotions like fear and anger. You will be able to remain calm and focused in otherwise stressful situations. When, on the other hand, you allow others to control your emotions, you are destined for failure.

In this chapter, we'll explore the ways that negative emotions can sabotage your athletic goals. We'll offer three tools for mastering your own psyche: self-talk (self-scripts), auto-suggestion, and visualization. These are similar yet distinct methods. While self-talk defines the attitudinal posture of your everyday thoughts and imagination, and self-scripts involve the recital of written or memorized "scripts," auto-suggestion seeks to stimulate the subconscious by having you repeat pre-conceived lines of thought in a calm, quiet, dimly lit environment. Visualization, on the other hand, entails the imagination's visual previewing of a forthcoming event. The use of these powerful complementary tools can distinguish one athlete from an equally gifted performer who is at the mercy of occasional negative emotions.

## Controlling Your Anger

In February 2015, Villanova's basketball team scored a lopsided (80–54) victory over Seton Hall. At a point when Villanova was winning by a large margin, Seton Hall's star player, Sterling Gibbs, struck Villanova's Ryan Arcidiacono in the face with a forearm. Seton Hall's coach suspended its leading scorer for two games. What is relevant in this situation was Gibbs's post-game reaction. He offered Arcidiacono an apology on Twitter, saying, "That's not who I am. My emotions got the best of me and that wasn't acceptable at all." Arcidiacono responded in kind on Twitter: "Emotions sometimes get the best of us, heat of the moment thing." As you can see from this story, even seasoned athletes sometimes have trouble dealing with adversity or defeat.

John Danaher, the head professor at the Renzo Gracie Academy, notes that anger "just makes people inefficient. Their breathing gets shallow, [and] they're too muscularly tense." Danaher goes on to say that "anger can take you away from your goal. You can get caught up in a desire for revenge, which distracts you." The key is to maintain focused poise. Those who achieve this state enter competitions without anxiety and fear. They possess a mentality of absolutely never thinking negatively or giving up, regardless of the odds. Athletes who successfully manage their anger can enjoy great success. For example, during an NBA game, Darrick Martin of the Grizzlies began trash-talking to Michael Jordan of the Chicago Bulls. Instead of giving in to his anger or trying to retaliate, Jordan gathered himself and went on a scoring rampage, lifting the Bulls to victory. Martin spent the remainder of the game on the bench.

*Controlled* anger can be a great motivator, like it was for Michael Jordan. Uncontrolled anger can propel you right out of the zone. A crucial first step in learning to manage your anger is to understand where it comes from. Gillian Butler and Tony Hope, in their book *Managing Your Mind,* note that our emotions are dominated by our thought process. Anger, for example, often can spring from a perception of being disrespected, unfairly judged, or exploited. A negative emotion such as anger can rise to the surface more easily when you are feeling exhausted or rushed. So when you are in the throes of anger, or even rage, it's critical to learn strategies to calm yourself.

To get an idea of what calm focused presence looks like, view online the demeanor of Yannick Agnel just before the start of the London 2012 Olympic 200-meter freestyle swim final.

## Self-Talk

Always be in control of your emotions. How do you accomplish this? The strategy of self-talk is a straightforward first step. When emotions such as anger and fear flare up, you can employ the self-talk method to calm yourself down.

To do this, talk to yourself (silently or audibly). Repeat inspiring words and phrases often, so your mind and subconscious will store them permanently. If, by chance, this type of regimen is not workable, choose the lyrics and melody of a favorite song.

Day in and day out, delete all random negative thoughts from your mind. Correct yourself each time you hear something debilitating come into your mind or out of your mouth. These are among the things you must do to ensure success at a high competitive level.

When in the throes of fear, anger, doubt, or rage, you are sometimes not capable of summoning the calmness needed for self-control and self-talk. In such a case, take a number of deep breaths, lower your shoulders, calm yourself down, and dispel all incapacitating thoughts. Say to yourself: "I control my thoughts and emotions. All I care about is performing at my best without distraction. I am now supremely confident about my abilities."

Consider an example of how you might utilize self-talk to control temptation. Imagine that you have finished a healthy meal following a strenuous workout. The restaurant/deli where you find yourself offers its customers free ice cream and nuts. Your mind and appetite begin to convince yourself that it is fine to consume a free dessert. After all, you've worked hard! Surely you've earned it, right? This is where self-talk comes into play. Stop for a moment, breathe easily, and reconsider with thoughts such as: "Who am I? What do I want to be? Do I want to compromise my training principles? Do I give in now, knowing that if I resist my desire, I will feel great and in a very short time (approximately twenty minutes) I won't even feel hungry for a dessert of any kind at all?"

Or consider another example, this one about overcoming anger. Imagine that your coach has singled you out to sit on the bench because of erratic, below-par play on your part. You can hardly believe it. You sit with anger beginning to boil over. *What did I do to deserve this?* you ask yourself. *It's not like the other players aren't screwing up too.*

Stop! Calm yourself; relax. Begin your self-talk. Make sure it is positive! Some athletes' self-talk sounds more like trash talk aimed at themselves or others. For example, psychologist David Stoop warns of "overgeneralization," "personalization," and "magnification" as psychological tendencies that make us pessimistic and stressed. When we overgeneralize, we see negative patterns where none actually exist ("That coach *always* benches me!"). When we personalize, we think the whole world is out to get us, and when we magnify, we make mountains out of molehills. All of these thwart our ability to maintain a healthy, optimistic attitude with the help of self-talk.

If you've been put on the bench, you can change the situation by remembering that the elite or aspiring athlete does not sulk or direct emotional anger at the coach. Rapidly, you (1) redirect your attention to the game; (2) encourage those who are playing; (3) resolve to be the best you can be once you are called back into the game; and (4) accept, humbly, the criticism behind having been benched. When you are back in play, you are refreshed mentally and physically and focused on success regardless of the score. In particular, you are loose and free of tension caused by anger, imagined humiliation, and taking yourself way too seriously in response to a necessary coaching move. What does the good coach want? Does he or she want to punish? No. He or she desires to afford you a moment of respite and reevaluation—in essence, a moment of positive self-talk.

Before concluding, one more word on the nature of self-talk. In essence, we are continually "talking" to ourselves. We are constantly reflecting on how we relate to what is happening around us as well as what our memory and random thinking brings into our consciousness. For example, it is normal for a college athlete to occasionally recollect his high-school athletic exploits. Without consciously perceiving it, the athlete is thus repeatedly calling to mind thoughts and images that reinforce his identification with athletic greatness. The mind of this model performer often remembers and "sees" the five touchdowns or goals scored in a single competitive encounter. Therefore, self-talk extends to the daily flow of ideas and images related to peak sport performance. They shape what we call our "disposition." As alluded to earlier, the high-performing athlete should block out random thinking of a negative nature. Thus, the flow of naturally uncontrolled thought remains positive.

## Self-Scripts

Another effective way to control debilitating emotions like anger and rage is to write "self-scripts" for how you will handle them, and ones for how you will want to eat, hydrate, train, and compete. Writing and reading self-scripts is analogous to audibly or silently repeating self-talk passages or thoughts. As with self-talk, self-scripts are texts that, ideally, capture in written form certain sensations, perceptions, or thoughts. Before embarking on a multi-week cycle of an off-season training plan, for example, write down the optimal experience you envision. This self-script should include lines that define how you would like to feel before and during workouts. The self-script can prepare your mind and body to reach and withstand certain pain thresholds that are the product of a well-conceived master training plan.

Whenever your mind begins to struggle, repeat your self-talk and self-script passages over and over until the mind believes them reflexively. To achieve greatness, the mental aspect of training and competing is essential. The truth is that most top-tier athletes share similar physical qualities. As already mentioned, what distinguishes one from the other is the mental control (disposition) they possess in critical situations.

Superior athletes, for example, do not lose composure when they are behind in a competition, are part of a team that is underperforming, or are criticized by a coach or referee. On the contrary, these types of situations will bring out the best in superior athletes. Why? Simply put, because they control and neutralize adversity through self-talk and the repetition of memorized self-scripts. Whatever the particular circumstances, these star individuals continue to perform at the height of their ability. Sulking, becoming angry, feeling defeated, or giving up are not part of their modus operandi. Elite athletes don't dwell on mistakes; they learn from them and then let them go.

In a high-stakes competitive situation, who remains composed and focused? In the Super Bowl, in a heavyweight world boxing championship, in the Olympic Wrestling Trials, who are the individuals who remain calm and determined, despite the pressured atmosphere? In Roman antiquity, gladiators (mostly slaves) were far from sharing the same attitude when facing death. Some offered little resistance in the arena, experiencing a quick demise. Others fought bravely throughout the mandatory five-year occasional exposure to death. (The best gladiators did not enter the arena very often.) The most successful gladiators exhibited the qualities of the Roman legions: unswerving commitment to rigorous training (which, surprisingly, included swimming), ability to endure drawn-out campaigns, contempt for the ever-present possibility of loss or death, and a love of glory. To a significant extent, today's warrior-athlete shares the above traits.

## Auto-suggestion

Let us take a moment to explain how auto-suggestion, a sister method to self-talk and self-scripts, works. Paul C. Jagot, in *Méthode Pratique d'Autosuggestion*, introduces his method with these words:

> The individual who desires to arrive at self-mastery should repeat the following whenever possible: "I am able to arrive at complete mastery over myself. . . . I possess the means to dominate myself. Every day, in every way, self-mastery takes

hold more and more solidly. I am my own master. My belief in these words marks the modification of my personality."

Think about this. We actually give ourselves subconscious auto-suggestions all the time. The trick here is to turn that around so that you do it *consciously*: you control the message. Experts say that the best approach to auto-suggestion is as follows:

1) Begin with a calm setting and frame of mind, preferably in a darkened space. Since auto-suggestion works though the subconscious, it is best to find yourself in a receptive psychic state, one free of all tension, both physical and mental. Closed eyes help produce a meditative mood apt at communicating to the subconscious mind whatever desires or goals you've chosen to fulfill.

2) Think carefully about the goals that you want to prioritize for auto-suggestion. For example, a 100-meter swimmer might decide on the following: "My body will travel effortlessly and smoothly on a downhill trajectory across the pool. My flip turn and push off the wall will resemble a torpedo launch or shark moving at top speed, as I powerfully gain more ground on my competitors. My powerful closing strokes will propel me forward faster than I have ever gone." As the swimmer is repeating the above, she is vividly picturing her body moving through the water, exhibiting ideal form and dominant, explosive speed. By "vividly" we mean that you should include all of the five senses (sight, sound, smell, taste, and touch) in your auto-suggestive thoughts.

3) Repeat your auto-suggestive, goal-oriented texts several times without distractions or thinking about anything else. Focus your mind exclusively on the *idea*. Your mind might be most receptive to auto-suggestion upon waking and before bedtime, so engage in the practice during those times as often as possible.

4) Tell yourself that "This thing is coming." It is going to come true. Your goal will be achieved. And when you are in competition or any kind of crunch time, bring your auto-suggestion to mind. When our swimmer is about to stand on the starting block, for example, she can execute

a final repetition of her self-talk passage. No noise, no commotion, nothing whatsoever can distract her from producing her indomitable best.

5) Expect success. As French psychotherapist Emile Coué says, "When the subconscious accepts this suggestion and transforms it into autosuggestion, the thing or things [ideas] are realized in every particular. . . . If you persuade yourself that you can do a certain thing, provided this thing is possible, you will do it, however difficult it may be."

In the following paragraphs, we illustrate auto-suggestive discourse at work in three different contexts: confronting anxiety, motivating yourself for an off-season workout, and preparing your mind for a day of competition.

*For confronting anxiety:* "I close my eyes and I feel a void, a detachment from the worries and general anxiety I sometimes feel. I will maintain this feeling of inner peace, no matter what is going on around me. In this state I am able to see more clearly, and to resolve mentally, problems that have led to bouts of debilitating anxiety in the past. I now feel free, calm, and creatively positive. Nothing will shake my resolve to continue to embrace this state. The smile now on my face is positive proof that I am free of anxiety and worry. Whatever this day holds, I will instinctively know how to comport myself with resolve, integrity, and good will."

*For an off-season workout:* "I close my eyes and rehearse a purposeful attitude toward my upcoming workout. As I move from one exercise to another I will maintain the concentration necessary to complete each with the proper form and at the ideal speed. The pain and burn I will feel are welcome signs of working out optimally. I believe that my workout victories will ensure a powerful performance during regular season competition. I feel enthusiasm grip my being. I believe these things and happily repeat this text to prime my workouts."

*For a competition day:* "Today, all my hard, sometimes painful, work will pay off. In a moment I will go over my specific role in detail in the upcoming event. Now, however, I close my eyes and feel tremendous confidence based on my hard work in preparation for this particular competition. I feel a quiet resolve in all my being. I feel that as the competition nears I will be ready to explode with energy that will not be denied. No matter the specific situation or score, I will be irrepressible. Now, I will mentally go over my assignments and strategies. Previous training guides me. I will picture vividly each basic move I will make during the competition. I truly feel unbeatable in my mind."

## KEY TAKEAWAYS

- To be a fully realized or elite athlete you must be able to control your own mind. A critical factor differentiating two athletes with the same athletic abilities is one's capacity to remain calm and focused in critical adversarial situations.

- Use self-talk and self-scripts to control fear, anger, and other negative emotions. Moreover, monitor your thought patterns to eliminate negative thinking.

- Auto-suggestion is a mind-control tool similar to self-talk and self-scripts. Use it when you are sitting in an armchair, totally relaxed, with your eyes closed. Repeat, silently or audibly, language that reflects your deepest desires and goals.

# 2

# Visualization

*Extraordinary people visualize not what is possible or probable,*
*but rather what is impossible. And by visualizing the impossible,*
*they begin to see it as possible.*

—Chérie Carter-Scott

**AT THE 1988 OLYMPICS IN SEOUL,**
American Tae Kwon Do competitor Dana Hee was badly injured going into the Games. "My back injury could not be helped, and I could not train," she explained later. "If I could not train during those final weeks, I stood no chance of winning. Well, I did train—in my mind. I used visualization to practice the movements, the timing—everything. By the time my competition came around, my back was rested enough to allow me to compete, and my mind made up for what I lacked physically." It was a rough path, but Hee won the gold medal, in part because she could rely on visualization when physical workouts were not possible.

In recent decades, great advances have been made in record athletic performances through scientists' study of the human mind and body. The speed, strength, endurance, and agility of professional athletes have all been improved through these enhancements. To promote and maintain an advantage over the competition, many athletes work closely with a team of experts, including trainers, doctors, physiologists, and sport psychologists. Not all athletes, however, are able to afford their own team of "experts." For the avid athlete or the athletic youngster with true potential to progress to the next level, a technique called "visualization" is a powerful psychological tool used across the globe. It can easily be incorporated into your training regimen to enhance performance.

Visualization is easy to learn; it does not discriminate on the basis of age, gender, skill level, or sport; it is free. For younger athletes, including those in high school, it may be best for an informed coach or parent to guide them through the actual visualization process until they have a firm understanding of what it is and how it works. This chapter provides some ideas for getting started with visualization as well as mastering it.

## Why Visualize?

Some athletes have a superficial knowledge of visualization but dismiss its effectiveness since it does not coincide with an active physical participation in the athlete's chosen sport. To the skeptics we would humbly say: Give it a try over a several-week period. Stay with it. No successful athlete would deny that "practice makes perfect." As long as you are able to concentrate, you can put visualization to successful use the first time you try it. After all, you are simply imagining as vividly as possible something with which you are normally quite familiar.

Visualization prepares your mind and body to perform at peak levels. For example, Sara, a champion skier, after studying the layout of the course on foot, visualizes her descent in the downhill over and over until the course holds no more surprises. By the time she is ready to ski in the actual competition, Sara has repeatedly imagined a rapid descent, including turns, jumps, and inevitable bumps in order to maximize performance. Her competitors who have not used the visualization technique are, by contrast, unpleasantly surprised at critical points of their descent because they do not "know" the course well enough. They are unable to anticipate

DeShaun, a high school basketball player, visualizes jump shooting from every spot on the imaginary court. He visualizes body elevation, smooth release, and the proper arc of the ball. By "seeing" the ball dropping through the basket without touching the rim, DeShaun is conditioning his mind and body for successful shooting during the actual game. The more realistic the process, the more vivid the imagery, and the more the five senses (sound, smell, sight, touch, and taste) are involved in his visualization, the better. For example, DeShaun hears the sound of the basketball snap through the net, followed by the roar of the crowd.

## Imagine It, Live It

What we imagine (believe) to be true is a powerful motivational mechanism in our daily lives. As Dr. Maxwell Maltz points out, what we imagine about ourselves, physically and psychologically, rules our behavior. Our nervous system, he says, "cannot tell the difference between an actual experience and one that is vividly imagined." Therefore, the goal of visualization is to trick our nervous system into believing we have physically accomplished what we have imagined in our minds.

In sports, practicing positive imaging is vital in attaining elite status. In a nutshell, while what we call "will" is crucial, the imagination is also vital in setting and attaining goals. Why is this the case? Because what you believe or imagine to be true about yourself, your team, and your opponent shapes the manner in which you will perform in competition.

Dr. Maltz refers to a study in which wide-awake college students were asked to imagine that one of their hands was plunged in ice water. Temperature readings of the hand in question were then taken and found to be low compared to the free hand. So, again, the principle at work here is as follows: What you imagine or believe to be true about yourself will guide you in the formation of goals and how you go about achieving them.

If an athlete imagines herself to be superior, automatic psychic and neural components will kick into action to make the imagined edge a reality. The mental pictures we carry around with us will determine our attitudes. Said another way, if we clearly and repeatedly imagine something about ourselves, our nervous system cannot differentiate between what is being imagined and reality itself. Therefore, if we imagine ourselves to be successful on the playing field, court, or in the pool, that success is much more likely to occur in reality.

Belief is key. In the quest for a sub-two-hour marathon, for example, Alex Hutchinson attributes the unparalleled success of East African runners chasing the sub-two-hour marathon time to the their belief that one day one of their own will break the two-hour barrier. The world record time has been inching down for years and is now 2:02:57, thanks to Kenyan marathoner Dennis Kimetto. Bringing it down even further, to below two hours, would require squeezing out an extra six and a half seconds per mile, but the Kenyans have faith that they will accomplish it. Hutchinson concludes: "Whoever finally runs a sub-two-hour marathon will have to start with the belief that it's possible; that he's the one to do it." Of course, most Kenyan runners, both men and women, grew up running long distances at high altitude (5,000 to 7,000 feet) to and from school, twice a day because of lunch. They were always on their feet helping their family survive under difficult circumstances. There is no doubt that the elite class of modern Kenyan runners motivate themselves by fueling their imagination with vivid pictures of their daily childhood experiences.

Visualization can help athletes take their success to the next level. Arnold Schwarzenegger (who was a professional bodybuilder before he became an action hero and politician) tells the story of a weightlifter who used visualization to control his mind and body. One day in the gym, Franco Columbu was unable to rise following a squat with five hundred pounds on his shoulders. Subsequently, a number of young Italian Americans entered the gym to see their hero, Franco. Fearing that the gathered fans would return to their respective neighborhoods disappointed that Franco could not handle the five-hundred-pound weight, Franco went outside to gather himself mentally. He returned and went on to do eight reps in front of the small crowd.

Schwarzenegger's own progress, before attaining universal renown, was fueled by visualizing the transformation of his body into one that looked like his idol, Reg Park. "I believed that one day I would be huge too. I would imagine it happening every time I trained at the gym and every night in bed, just before I fell asleep," Schwarzenegger said. "I am convinced that you become what you think about most. Dwell on the negative and you fail. Dwell on positive thoughts and you succeed. . . . Success will be yours [if you use] the power of your mind to its fullest potential. Then nothing can stop you."

Interestingly, Schwarzenegger continually writes articles in bodybuilding magazines on the theme of visualization. Specifically, he has noted the fact that he is a visual learner and that the day he picked up a bodybuilding magazine with Reg Park's picture on the cover was the day he began to obsessively visualize himself as a future Mr. Universe (like Reg Park). The picture of Reg Park in Schwarzenegger's mind was his great motivator.

Visualization helped professional golfer Jack Nicklaus, who essentially played each shot twice: once in his imagination and a second time in the tournament. In _Golf My Way_, Nicklaus said, "I never hit a shot, not even in practice, without having a sharp, in-focus picture of it in my head. It's like a color movie. [ … ] I see the ball going there, even its behavior on landing."

Specific detail is an important component of visualization. Author Gary Mack recounts how Pelé prepared for every soccer match: "An hour before he stepped out onto the field, Pelé went into the locker room and retreated to a private corner, towels over his head. Then he began to roll his mental camera. [ … ] He saw himself dribbling through defenders, heading shots and scoring goals." Again, visualizing in vivid detail is often the elite athlete's pre-competition way to ensure the best subsequent outcome possible.

## Training Your Mind through Visualization

At first glance, visualization may strike an uninformed athlete as being a type of hypnosis. This is not the case. Visualization is indeed a practice and discipline of the mind, but only a yoga guru, or the like, is able to achieve an out-of-this-world self-hypnotic state. What you as an athlete can realize is a comfortable meditative state during which you vividly imagine yourself executing perfectly a specific aspect of your sport, whether that be a triple axel, a high jump, a three-point shot, or a more elaborate performance such as a giant slalom. A faulty understanding of the visualization technique, and its subsequent dismissal, strips you of the opportunity to become faster, stronger, more accurate, and more solidly grounded in the fundamentals of your chosen sport.

In practical terms, how does visualization work? Let's apply visualization to a pre-game football situation involving a defensive back, Noah. The evening before the game, Noah sits in an easy chair, eyes closed, imagining the different formations of the opposing team and the correct way he has been trained to respond to them. Part of the clear mental picture he focuses on involves anticipating the movement of the wide receivers and picturing himself stepping in at the right moment and angle to intercept the ball. Likewise, Noah "sees" himself running side by side with the offensive player, preventing the quarterback from throwing his way. Ideally, Noah visually runs through the entire offensive package of the opponent and, consequently, feels supremely confident before he goes to bed. He may repeat a shortened version of the above before game time.

Fitness guru Mario Lopez offers an interesting and effective variation of the visualization method defined above. Lopez has an athlete close her eyes, inhale slowly through the nose and exhale through the mouth. Then she concentrates on how she felt after her last great workout and chooses a word such as "power" or "explosiveness" to evoke the workout in question. After repeating the word three times, she imagines one full set of an exercise she is presently going to do, one rep at a time. She mentally associates the past "great feeling" she's just conjured with each of the reps she is about to perform. Lastly, she also "sees" the ideal body shape the exercise set is meant to produce. This mental exercise is designed to "fiercely energize" her for another great workout.

When you visualize, you are making connections between your brain and your muscles. Of course, each sport utilizes different muscles and muscle groups, and the process of visualization can be tailored to any of them. You can use this technique to improve in any area of a sport. By developing a neural path between the brain and the muscles you use in your sport, those muscles become more accustomed to acting in the appropriate way. Then when you engage in the actual movement, the muscles will "remember" the correct way to move.

For an action that is more complicated, be sure to visualize the correct way to execute it, or you can do more harm than good. If you throw a football awkwardly and visualize the movement the same way, you are building faulty neural pathways and reinforcing bad habits.

## Other Visual Techniques

Another approach to successful visualization entails repeatedly watching great athletes performing online and internalizing their movements. For middle distance runners, for example, it would prove beneficial to observe Joaquim Cruz of Brazil running the 800 meters as well as Hicham El Guerrouj of Morocco running the 1,500 meters. The powerful yet fluid stride of these two athletes is exemplary. On the women's side, the overall form of 400-meter runner Marie-José Pérec of France is a thing of beauty. For sprint swimmers, we recommend watching closely the dissimilar but highly effective styles of Russia's Alexander Popov and Florent Manaudou of France.

The calm environment we recommend when going through the visualization process may remind you of meditation. In fact, our experience practicing visualization does resemble meditation in that the mind and body tend to relax. The anxiety you may feel preceding a challenging competition tends to decrease, even disappear. Why is that? Because, as in Noah's case, visualization prepares the mind and body to meet an upcoming challenge with enhanced confidence. Visualizing how, in detail, you handle a difficult or strenuous situation (high intensity training, for example) will necessarily decrease stress and increase confidence.

## KEY TAKEAWAYS

- Before a workout or competition, the ability to visualize a perfect performance significantly enhances the outcome of the actual workout or competition.

- The more detailed and more vivid the imagery, the more successful you will be. Make it a habit to insert the five senses (sound, smell, sight, touch, and taste) into the visualization scenario.

- Remember to dispel negative thinking patterns. Your mind is constantly awash with thoughts of all kinds. By being aware of which ones are negative, you can slowly block them. In time, these thoughts will enter the mind less and less often.

# 3

# The Outside World Does Not Control Our Thoughts

*Men [and women] are disturbed, not by things,*

*but by the view they take of them.*

—Epictetus

**SOMETIMES THE ELITE ATHLETE FINDS** it difficult to transition from high school to the college level. As we shall see, the reason behind the lack of success in college often turns out to be purely psychological: a lack of self-confidence fueled by negative thinking. In this chapter, we will define ways to maintain focus and bolster your self-confidence despite surrounding negative circumstances. Aspiring athletes may have superior physical talents such as natural coordination, agility, speed, strength, endurance, and so on. However, if in late adolescence they begin to suffer from debilitating psychological moods, they will have problems achieving athletic greatness in college and beyond. In fact, if the psychological component of their overall makeup proves to be somewhat weak—no matter how swift, explosive, or talented they may be athletically—the result will be ultimate failure or, at best, mediocre achievement.

This chapter argues that you can influence your mood by monitoring your train of thought. You can accomplish this by not obsessing over problems that are beyond your control, letting go of negative thoughts and memories, accepting your environment, and living vibrantly in the present.

In the final analysis, you control your psychological outlook, mood, and beliefs. If your thoughts are full of inspired content, they will produce states of exhilaration, excitement, and a host of similar feelings that will prepare you well for a workout or competition. We have seen how self-talk, auto-suggestion, and visualization condition the mind to produce the emotional motivation behind extraordinarily successful training and superior competitive results. Now let's focus on four positive mental habits that will keep you on the right track.

## Don't Obsess over Problems You Can't Control

Sometimes, people don't respond well to chance external stimuli. Let us imagine, for example, that a college baseball standout named Ray approaches his car on his way to the grocery store. As he opens the driver-side door he notices a deep scratch on the vehicle's body—a scratch that was not there previously. Once in the car, Ray's eyes fall on the gas gauge, which signals the car is almost out of fuel. Furthermore, the engine service light is on. A short while later, Ray goes grocery shopping and fills the back of his car with grocery bags. At home, as he opens the hatchback, some of the grocery bags fall to the pavement and their contents spill everywhere.

In reaction, the weak mind will say to itself: "Oh, things are going badly. I'm having a bad day. I don't feel like going to the gym anymore." Many of us would do the same, and allow external circumstances to derail our plans for a rigorous workout at the gym after the ill-fated trip to the grocery store. Ray, however, is philosophical. "These and other chance-driven occurrences are part of everyday life," he reminds himself. "I choose to ignore any impact they could have on my mind and will remain upbeat. In fact, I will take care of these insignificant problems right away and then hit the gym."

Ray's reaction is a model of how trained athletes can choose to prevent circumstances that are outside their control from dominating their psyche. When you are experiencing a "bad day" (car trouble, traffic, another person's rudeness, never receiving a call or text you were expecting, etc.), the truth is that you have to dismiss it. If problems of a practical nature arise by chance (computer problems, and the like), try to take care of them immediately. By acting decisively and promptly, you eliminate nagging stress and are free to work out with a clear focus, moving ahead in a positive and productive frame of mind.

It is true that some circumstances can be particularly stressful, but it's not helpful to let anxiety derail you. Rather, make contingency plans and figure out a suitable solution.

## Let Go of Negative Thoughts

Sometimes, athletes who do not have a problem dealing with outside circumstances can get caught up in spirals of negative thinking that damage their chances of success. It takes a great deal of focused mental energy to overcome those mental patterns. Consider the story of Henry, a truly gifted offensive back who was a football star in high school but then found himself second at his position on the depth chart of a prominent college team. When originally faced with the fact that he would be second-string, Henry was so psychologically and emotionally shaken that he thought seriously about transferring to another college, even though he understood that this would mean losing a year of eligibility in the process.

What did Henry, a quiet, reflective individual, ultimately decide to do? He stayed put. His parents lived nearby, and he could see his steady girlfriend regularly. Moreover, the handsome Henry was a fan favorite. Deep down, Henry secretly burned with one overriding thought: "No matter what it takes, no matter how much time elapses, I will ultimately prevail; that is, I will not only become a starter, but will ultimately become recognized as one of the NFL's finest backs." To arrive at this state of mind Henry first had to calm down. He called upon every mind-control strategy he knew (especially self-talk, auto-suggestion, and visualization) to remain whole, psychologically speaking. Instead of giving in to his initial thoughts and moods that included sulking, blaming everyone in sight (particularly the head coach), and asking himself why he should continue to work so hard, Henry, on his own, began to tell himself that he would eventually prove everyone wrong: As a great professional player he would make everyone wonder why he'd once had to share halfback duties with another admittedly outstanding player.

You may be asking yourself what is so virtuous about burning psychologically with what sound like thoughts of revenge. But it was not the dangerous and futile emotion of aggressive revenge that dominated Henry's psyche, but a healthy, powerful drive to continue to develop his physical and psychological attributes. In every practice and game he sought to reinforce his conviction that as a professional he would shine. Yes, Henry was human. Part of his motivation was a desire to prove certain individuals wrong in their judgment; however, once he had thought things through, he made sure that his entire being was focused primarily on physical, psychological, and moral improvement. As a college senior, his talents were so evident that an outside observer would conclude that he was "sharing" the backfield duties pretty much equally with the other outstanding back. Henry regularly visualized himself as an irrepressible, smoothly agile, yet powerful runner, whose attributes would one day be fully recognized. Whenever doubt knocked at his door, Henry would automatically use self-talk to make doubt an unwelcome intruder.

Henry went on to be drafted by an NFL team in the sixth round but turned out to be an All-Pro performer for quite a number of years. Steadfastness, a belief in himself, and hard work paid off handsomely. The moral of his story is that no matter what negative, external circumstances surround an elite athlete, he or she is "free" to think optimistic thoughts which, in turn, lead to strikingly powerful performances.

## Accept Your Environment

Some athletes don't have difficulty thinking positive thoughts about themselves. However, they are critical of the people and the settings around them. Jennifer, a college soccer star, works out at a fitness center in the off-season. Jennifer does not like the type of music always playing on the loudspeaker; she does not appreciate the fact that the women who work out when she is there do not make the effort to say hello to her; and finally, she doesn't care for the woman at the check-in desk. Instead of concentrating on the training session at hand, Jennifer spends quite a bit of time and mental energy thinking negatively about the fitness center her college athletic department has assigned her to because of the special equipment found there.

One day, Jennifer shares her criticisms with her mother on the phone. Her mother listens with care, pauses, and then replies: "Jennifer, I'd like you to try what I'm about to say. When you walk into the fitness center, smile at the woman clerk and say a big 'Hello, how are you doing today?' Once inside, whenever you run into one of the women you believe is distant, say hello with a smile. And finally, forget about the music. You can bring your own whenever you like." Jennifer does as her mother has suggested and as if by magic, the imagined cold atmosphere of the fitness center is transformed into a warm, inviting space.

It's important to stop wasting time bemoaning your environment and start looking for ways to adapt to it. In life, situations like those surrounding Jennifer will materialize periodically. They are inevitable. Outstanding high-school, college, or pro athletes possess the intellectual means to step back calmly, study a troublesome situation, and implement a "winning" solution to the problem at hand, be it psychological or practical.

The psychology of Krishnamurti (1895–1986) can be quite helpful when you have the feeling that things in your day, or life in general, are going badly or that the world is against you. Krishnamurti wrote extensively of his desire to free humankind from fears of all kinds. He sought to liberate men and women from what he perceived to be the enveloping chains of a stressed, conformist society.

Let us imagine an athlete, Jeannette, who is convinced that she habitually is subject to bad luck. Were Krishnamurti to counsel Jeannette, he would tell her the following. "First, calm down, relax, and regulate your breathing to eliminate physiological and psychic tension. Now close your eyes. Are you experiencing any physical pain? Are you physically healthy? Can you smile and realize that regardless of what problematic events (most of which are beyond your control) are somehow affecting you, they need not adversely disturb your right to remain composed and serene?"

Of course, a breakup, divorce, or a death in the family, among other challenging events, are of such a psychologically painful nature that it does take some considerable amount of time for individuals to heal. That having been said, as regards everyday common occurrences of an irritating nature, there is no reason for you not to remain positive and impervious to anxiety.

## Live Vibrantly in the Present

So, in conclusion, you should habitually remain aware of the full array of mind-control solutions you possess to overcome whatever problem—large or small, sports-related or not—that presents itself. Whether the problem is of a practical or psychological nature does not matter. Calmly, thoughtfully, and with self-confidence apply one or more of the mind-related solutions outlined above to whatever may be trying to slow you down on your way to full potential or elite sport status.

## KEY TAKEAWAYS

- When things are not going well for us, we have a tendency to believe that we are somehow responsible for circumstances that, in reality, are purely chance-driven and totally unrelated to ourselves.

- Instead of giving in to negative thoughts, re-channel them into positive ones. We have a good deal of control over what we think; we can interpret potentially troubling situations in a healthy, productive manner.

- Practice accepting and adapting to your environment rather than complaining about it.

# 4

# Body Language and Body Control

*Our body language expresses our mental state whether we like it or not. Our facial expressions, voice, posture, and all the other components of body language reflect our mental and emotional condition every second.*

—Olivia Fox Cabane

**IN 2014, A FACIAL CODING EXPERT** was called in to evaluate players from various professional football teams to better assess the value of potential draft choices. Such experts claim that close analysis of facial expression and body language can tell them which players will succeed and which won't, and whether they will be a pleasure to work with or turn out to be "locker room poison" for the rest of the team. Jeff Foster, who runs the NFL Scouting Combine, scrutinized the qualities of quarterbacks and safeties in particular. Foster asserts that facial coding methods are capable of "picking apart the psyches of potential [high draft] picks" and helping teams decipher which draft candidates display a champion's heart in adverse conditions. In the case of Robert Griffin III, formerly of the Washington Redskins, the raised eyebrows and subsequent closed-eye fatigue displayed in post-game interviews illustrated "intense discontent" and a lack of "faith in how things are being handled [in

Washington]." And Jay Cutler of the Chicago Bears demonstrated a wry, sarcastic smile that the consultant interpreted as "an aversion reaction, a kind of poor man's version of contempt except that contempt can also be indicative of confidence."

As an athlete, it is essential for you to have positive and strong body language, including facial expression. It is advantageous to look confident at all times, since perceptive opponents will pick up on fear and doubt, and turn them to their advantage. In this chapter we'll explore how your body language affects how other people perceive you, and offer tips on how to project composure and strength. We'll also address how positive body language can actually improve how you feel about yourself and your sport.

## Body Language Affects How Others See You

Imagine you're a basketball player in a "pre-game" situation. As you and the other team warm up on the court, what are you doing? Are you laughing it up? Missing layups out of inattention? Or are you focused, charged with a confident attitude? Are your shoulders back or already slumped in the defeat you worry will begin to occur when the game begins? The other team is watching you. What do they see?

Assertive body and facial languages are critical in athletics. Look at their importance in gymnastics. Not only are gymnasts asked to execute incredible displays of athleticism, but they must also maintain a consistently upbeat attitude, ever mindful that the judges are watching. They have to smile even after a poor routine or dismount although smiling could be the last thing they actually want to do. Body language doesn't talk; it screams.

You're skeptical? Let's look at some research. In one experiment, onlookers could "read" people's body language even when all they were seeing was dots on a screen, not the people themselves. "Researchers have shown that when watching a body's movements reduced to points of light on a screen, observers can still read grief, anger, joy, disgust, fear, and surprise," says Lior Suchard. "A research team led by Winand Dittrich at the University of Hertfordshire, England, worked with trained dancers to investigate just how easy it is to interpret emotion by reading body language only." The research results found that 88 percent of the participants were correct in discerning the emotions portrayed by the individual teams of dancers.

As Julius Fast repeatedly points out in the book *Body Language*, your facial expression, and how you walk, stand, sit, gesticulate, and project your voice, send out continuous messages related to your emotional state, deepest feelings, and hidden thoughts. There are several key signals that your body and facial expression give, even when you are not consciously aware of them. Bad body language, for example, is visible when an athlete's shoulders are scrunched up or slumped.

Even more than shoulder position, the most revealing feature of our body and facial language is the expression of our eyes. Floyd Patterson, the boxer, saw fear in the eyes of Ingemar Johansson just before their rematch. In the first bout Johansson had annihilated Patterson. But in the third round of the rematch, as we recount in detail later in this book, Patterson caught Johansson with a perfect left hook which left his adversary on the canvas for some minutes. Just before the opening bell, from the expression in Johansson's eyes, Patterson "knew" he would be the first heavyweight boxer in history to regain his crown.

As Patterson's story shows, eye contact can be very important between boxers before a fight. If your opponent is staring at you and you break eye contact first, it signals weakness. But this lesson applies to many other sports as well. If you have a staring contest with a rival athlete, look confident and exude signs of composure. This indicates that you have no fear. Even if you *are* scared, you can control your fear through positive self-talk. You call the shots. You are dominant at all times. Tell yourself to relax and breathe naturally. Know and repeat the thought that you have not compromised on your preparatory training and that for this particular contest you have done your best to pay attention to your coach and are at the optimal level of strength, speed, and endurance. Again, your psychological "will" to succeed is at one with your feelings and body language. Your competitive adversaries are observing and instinctively receiving signals from the way your carry yourself. Your eyes reflect this state and your opponents cannot help but notice your steely composure.

## Body Language Affects How You See Yourself

It's not just other people who are affected by your body language. You may not realize it, but your body language can determine how you view yourself. We've talked in this book about how our moment-to-moment thoughts can dictate how we feel, but it's also true that our body language can influence our thoughts and our feelings. Simply put, mental toughness requires positive body and facial language when a competition is not going well.

We can act our way into *right* thinking just as easily as we can think our way into *right* acting. Our personality often dictates our body language. Some people show little emotion or cannot even tell how they are actually feeling. On the opposite end, some athletes are incredibly energetic and visibly show their emotions after a well-executed move. This can intimidate an opponent. But when we are not performing well, body language often becomes supremely significant and can bring us into a downward spiral leading to defeat.

Our best advice is to fake it until you make it. We've all been there. It is downright painful when we don't perform well. Address your body language when you are not doing well in a competition. Try to show the same posture and facial expression as when you are competing optimally. Keep your head up, shoulders down and back, and try to encourage others, if team play is in question. Cheer or congratulate your teammates; hustle; remain composed and focused. Act the part and you will become the animator of positive emotion in adverse situations. Adversity will inspire elite athletes to excel. Body language and positive thinking will help bring you back to your naturally productive state.

In sports such as wrestling, golf, tennis, soccer, and baseball, among many others, there exist built-in pauses, short or long, during which adversaries scrutinize each other. Do not be influenced by what you believe you "see" in the comportment of opponents. Moreover, do not be impressed by the score or by what appears to be a losing situation. On the contrary, know that in sport competition, the obvious winner often loses, sometimes in the very last seconds of an encounter. So, do not interpret the opponent's confident body and facial signals as representing potential inevitable victory. Counter with supreme composure and the knowledge that you can overcome what, to weak individuals, appears to be a lost situation. Rally with all your heart and soul. Marvel at how things can turn your way when opponents least expect it.

## KEY TAKEAWAYS

- Body posture and facial expression constantly project your inner mood and attitude.

- Your opponent instinctively is able to "read" how confident or defeatist you are before and during a competition.

- Habituate yourself to project a "winning" attitude through body and facial language. Be unaffected by the score. On the contrary, produce your best when things momentarily look bleak.

# PART 2

# WORK ETHIC AND PHYSICAL TRAINING

# 5

# Work Ethic:
# Theory and Practice

*There may be people that have more talent than you, but there's no excuse for anyone to work harder than you do.*

—Derek Jeter

**IN 1959, LEGENDARY AUSTRALIAN** track coach Percy Wells Cerutty advised the readers of *Track & Field News* about what it took to be a champion. At that time, Cerutty's star protégé, Herb Elliott, had earned success on the world stage but had yet to achieve his ultimate goal: an Olympic gold medal. The following year, Elliott clinched the gold in the 1500 meters at the Rome Games, a testament to his own discipline and the winning strategies of his famous coach.

What were those strategies? As Cerutty pointed out, natural talent wasn't everything. In the beginning, world champion athletes aren't that different from everybody else. They might have an inherent physical "ability above the average," he said, but more important than natural athletic gifts was a sense of "innate worth." Great athletes didn't get discouraged easily. They were self-reliant, focused, and ambitious. And above all, they worked hard.

There is no substitute for daily work, Cerutty taught. Athletic training could be exhausting, even "soul-killing," but it was the only way to get an athlete "out of the rut" to become world class. "No one can do it for you; do your training and your thinking," he told readers. Coaches could motivate and strategize, but they could only point the way. What separated the truly great athletes from the rest was their ability to doggedly follow that path, treating every discouragement as a learning experience and setting goals that could only be achieved by grueling physical training.

Cerutty was correct. Every athlete needs to possess an irrepressibly strong work ethic. Without it, you will not be able to achieve the goals detailed in the ensuing chapters of this book. Some individuals may be blessed with an inherent proclivity to work hard, some learn it from their parents, and some must develop it. This chapter helps you learn how.

## The Fruit of a Strong Work Ethic

In the introduction to this book, I (David Hill) mentioned that I was not necessarily the most natural or talented athlete by birth. In fact I was a scrawny, slight teenager who could have been a model for the Charles Atlas ads of an earlier era. (For those of you who are way too young to be acquainted with Charles Atlas, let us say that he was the equivalent of Captain America—*before* Captain America got his superpowers.) In the Atlas advertising materials, the "skinny kid" gets sand thrown in his face, but then religiously follows the "Charles Atlas Method" and takes revenge. Well, we don't subscribe to being a bully or exacting revenge. However, a work ethic that includes sticking to a rigorous regimen will, over time, transform the "scrawny" athlete into a good or superior one and the gifted athlete into an elite performer.

Let us highlight one other example of what well-planned, sustained physical effort can do, even for the person with only a modicum of natural skills. In 2014, the *New York Times* reported the story of nineteen-year-old Olivia Prokopova, a native of the Czech Republic. *Olivia who?* You are asking. She is the world Mini Golf champion. Yes, you may be rolling your eyes or laughing a little, but her work ethic is no joke. "She's not that much better than the others; she just practices more," said Bob Detwiler, president of the US ProMiniGolf Association. A fellow traveler on the competitive circuit, Brad Lebo, put it another way: "There's always an infinite amount of information to learn, and Olivia's work ethic is extremely good. She sometimes goes to places several weeks in advance and charts out the course, and that gives her a big advantage." She practices for eight to twelve hours a day, six days a week, and also keeps up with schoolwork. Her training has been strenuous enough to require reparative surgery on both knees and one of her wrists. Humble about herself, she insists, "I haven't got any talent; I just practice every day." She explains her success with a single word: "diligence."

Self-discipline has been the key to Prokopova's achievements, including being the first person to ever win the triple crown of Mini Golf. Her rigorous daily preparation may seem unusual, but for elite athletes it's essential. In *No Excuses! The Power of Self-Discipline*, Brian Tracy defines the path to successful goal attainment as the ability to follow a pre-conceived plan in a timely manner, whether you feel like it or not. He adds, "Success is possible only when you can master your own emotions, appetites, and inclinations." Tracy concludes that "When you master the power of self-discipline, you will become unstoppable, like a force of nature," and promises that when this happens, "You will accomplish more in the next few months and years than most people accomplish in a lifetime."

That may seem like a grandiose, pie-in-the-sky guarantee, but we can tell you that with self-discipline and an unswerving work ethic, you can achieve far more than you would have dreamed possible. For the athlete, a positive work ethic affects every aspect of life, from how you organize your time to the food you put into your body (or try to avoid) to controlling your tongue when you're angry or discouraged. It means living according to a plan. And that means that first you have to decide upon that plan.

## Setting a Daily Training Schedule—and Sticking to It

Whatever your situation, the first thing you need to do to develop or enhance your work ethic is to create a long-term off-season work and rest schedule, and then stick to it. Normally, you do not fundamentally change the work schedule for any reason. If you begin to alter it, without a valid overriding reason, then it is not going to happen. In fact, your competitive identity is a reflection of how closely you manage to stick to the particulars of your training agenda. In the final analysis, only you will know to what degree you have remained faithful to the program.

Let us clarify an important point. Particularly in the early stages of your off-season workouts, it may be necessary to alter the established blueprint. Only experiencing the training regimen can tell you if certain changes are needed. For example—and this may sound contradictory—you may find that you are overtraining, and that sticking to the original plan is making you a chronically tired athlete. So, be honest with yourself. Train hard, but be sure to train smart.

Since this guide speaks to athletes at all levels, we are aware of the influence coaches and professional trainers can have on you. If your trainers and coaches are well informed and innovative in their ways, you are very fortunate and should listen carefully to what they tell you. In the case of heavyweight boxer Rocky Marciano in the 1950s, true success was elusive until Al Weill (manager) and Charley Goldman (trainer) began working for Marciano. Goldman was a gentle soul who was friendly with everyone he met, but he was not shy about suggesting improvements. In a self-assured and truly professional manner, one tinged with genius, he slowly retooled Marciano's awkward boxing stance and unconvincing training methods, and introduced a powerful left hook to Marciano's arsenal of punches. Marciano never lost a bout. He was the undefeated champion of the world from 1952 to 1956 and is considered one of the greatest boxers of all time.

What your personal workout plan looks like is going to vary according to your individual needs. How much time can you allot to training, and how can you increase it over the next few months? What weaknesses do you have that require the expenditure of extra workout time? Great athletes do not just work on what comes naturally to them, but allocate extra time to the things that do not. For example, the female gymnast who is already superb at vault and floor exercise trains for those particular events but also assigns extra hours to her two least favorite events, the uneven bars and the balance beam.

Think about the following questions as you cultivate your workout plan:

- What do you dream about?

- What images does your mind repeatedly evoke related to spectacular athletic performance?

- How do you picture yourself physically as you appear for your first team practice?

- Do you picture yourself performing in a manner such that your coaches and teammates take notice?

- Do you imagine being the unexpected center of attention?

- Do you see yourself performing at the highest levels, securing victory, and breaking records?

If the answer to all these questions is "Yes," you are on your way to reaching your full potential or attaining elite sport status. However, all the winning images that you project will not amount to very much unless you and your coach or trainer devise unusually effective workout strategies. Moreover, remember: Ascending to elite sport status or achieving your full potential as an athlete also entails carefully monitoring your nutritional, psychological, physical, and moral health.

It is vital to clearly define the goal; how, in detail, you intend to achieve it and in how much time. Of course, a highly competent coach or professional trainer, if available, would be the ideal architect of an off-season workout blueprint. Once the above-mentioned variables have been established, it is incumbent on you to ensure that each training session produces quality gains. This entails remaining focused throughout the workout rather than being easily distracted. Canadian Adam Kreek, a gold medalist in the 2008 Olympic rowing competition in Beijing, said, "I believe that the conscious presence in each moment is the golden key to effective practice. Practice is not going through the motions with our body while our mind and spirit reside elsewhere. Rather, practice is about focused effort with our entire being. This engrains habit and skill into our unconscious self."

In other words, make every practice count. Alexander Popov, multiple world and Olympic champion during the 1990s, regularly swam eighty to ninety miles a week. What defined his long practice swims was Popov's determination, believe it or not, to make each leg-and-arm crawl cycle either perfect or superior to prior efforts. Every single moment of his long swims was dedicated to decreasing drag. Spectators at one of his many competitions often remarked that Popov appeared to be swimming his 50- and 100-meter events in slow motion compared to the other swimmers. The reason: Popov glided through the water in a more efficient manner than his competitors. The fewer strokes he took, the longer the glide, and the more tenths of a second he dropped from his world records.

The substance of the daily training/rest agenda that you ultimately devise should be based on the best available input derived from books, websites, magazines, seminars, valid online insights, and the word of experts, successful athletes, and coaches. Smart training and total commitment to a work ethic entail the proper mix of carefully planned workouts and necessary rest periods. Adherence to a rigorous workout schedule does not mean that you should ignore proper, sustained sleep habits and rest days. On the contrary, sleep and rest days keep the mind and body fresh so that training remains something that can be fun and that you look forward to. Moreover, they ward off the dangerous state known as overtraining. The symptoms of this latter condition are chronic fatigue, sleep problems, diminished motivation, lack of appetite, unexplained weight loss, body aches, depressive symptoms, chronic colds, and overuse injuries. Inevitably, fatigue *will* be apparent on some mornings. However, with proper nutrition, rest, and mind control, occasional, but manageable fatigue will not prevent you from completing the work schedule on those particular days. Let it be said now that large-portion dinners, late-night snacks or attendance at night clubs are directly detrimental to remaining highly motivated upon rising. Excess, in general, makes recoverability from fatigue more problematic.

Within the context of creating a wise training agenda, keep in mind that you should build up your exercise regimen gradually. If you have taken a relatively long break following the competitive season, it is vital to warm up slowly, followed by stretching, before engaging in a strenuous workout. High intensity interval training (HIIT), spin classes, and other similar types of cardio exercises should not be undertaken without proper pre-conditioning, lasting several weeks. Deeper into the off-season you will slowly increase the volume and intensity of work. Long-distance running, the triathlon, and endurance events often call for covering one hundred or so miles a week at a relatively easy, aerobic pace. This type of training builds a pre-season aerobic base. Elite runners such as Mo Farah mix aerobic base-type running with twenty miles a week of tempo pace. As the competitive season looms on the horizon, volume should decrease in favor of accentuated intensity. Late in the pre-season schedule, sprinter Michael Johnson, under the watchful eye of Baylor University track coach Clyde Hart, would regularly limit interval training on certain days to two 600-meter runs at near-all-out pace. This kept the world's best 200- and 400-meter runner fresh before the competitive season entered its most demanding stage.

When you strictly follow an off-season training plan in swimming, wrestling, soccer, or any other cardio-intensive sport, and your blueprint is taxing and innovative, you will eventually experience a magical moment in the afterglow of prolonged successful training when you realize you have ascended to a new level; you are a rising star.

Ambitious athletes should be wary of specialized high-tech training centers that push people too hard and too fast. Self-discipline is vital, but it's unwise to imagine that merely having the will to do something is going to be enough if you haven't yet trained your body to achieve that goal. To simply decide to outwork every other athlete in your field all day long à la Dan Gable (of folkstyle and freestyle wrestling fame) will necessarily lead to overtraining—and therefore to injury. However, to read about and be inspired by Gable's out-of-this-world work ethic is a positive idea. A less extreme but effective work-ethic formula is evident in the philosophy of David Blatt, former basketball coach of the Cleveland Cavaliers. Growing up in a broken home, he was independent for his age and "extremely driven. I would get up earlier, try harder, practice harder, take any challenge more seriously than anyone else." His hard work paid off, first as an athlete and then as a winning coach. It can pay off for you, regardless of the sport in which you participate.

## Utilizing the Off-Season to Your Advantage

For the elite athlete, the off-season may initially serve as a period of rest. Following a long season, this is normal. Athletes need a moment of respite during which they can calmly reassess progress and study their relative position vis-à-vis other athletes, their progress over the season, their relationships with teammates and coaches, and so on. For athletes who are students, it is a time to ensure that studies and grades are in order. Overall, however, if you wish to be an elite or exceptional athlete, the off-season can also be a time of transformation. If you have a dedicated work ethic, it can be an exciting opportunity to improve physically and evolve emotionally.

Particularly in the off-season, if your coach-and-trainer-generated workout plans are not challenging enough or don't seem to fit your needs, you should determine the nature of your weaker physical and moral attributes (i.e., those related to strength, speed, endurance, explosiveness, agility, balance, mind control, and moral values) and do all in your power to devise cutting-edge means to improve upon them. For example, if you are a soccer player, you might set up increasingly charged mazes of obstacles through which you practice dribbling, timing each successful attempt. Having completed this phase of training, you could then find two willing teammates who attempt to steal the soccer ball as you proceed to dribble downfield toward a kick at the goal.

With the help of the detailed information present in the other chapters of this book, developing and implementing a rigorous work ethic during the off-season will help you achieve the goals you envision. Maintaining a commitment to a well-thought-out work plan (i.e., sticking to a schedule) can be secured more easily with the help of the mind control techniques we have already discussed, such as self-talk, self-scripts, auto-suggestion, and visualization. Mind control is the fundamental element in the production of an enduring, unaltered workout schedule. Mind control needs to be practiced every day; otherwise, the blueprint outlining training, eating, drinking and resting risks changes that are detrimental. Commitment to each day's schedule—assuming the latter is based on the best available expertise—is a must. Often modifying the schedule because you "don't feel like training" means that you possess poor self-discipline.

Let us consider the example of Willis, a college sophomore basketball center. He is six feet, eleven inches tall and is relatively muscular, with decent natural coordination. So far in his college career, he has not made a big impression on the coaching staff and, therefore, has not played very many minutes during the past season. Mostly, Willis has observed each pre-season and regular season game from the bench. Hopefully, he has learned quite a bit about strategy and performance through observation from that perspective. Now the season is over. The head coach has outlined an off-season training regimen, and the strength coach has created a personalized series of workouts intended to make him stronger. This is all fine and good. However, Willis possesses a burning desire to come out from under the shadow of being a second- or third-string player.

He's not satisfied with the general perceptions that his coach and teammates harbor vis-à-vis his performance, and he's going to exploit the extended free time that the off-season provides in order to change those perceptions and also impress the fans who assiduously attend games. Because of his fierce desire to improve dramatically, Willis will not take much time off, post-season. His mind is bubbling over with secret ambitions unsuspected by teammates and coaches. He has scoured bookstores and the Internet, spoken with coaches and trainers, and carefully studied which off-season strategy to follow in order to return next year as a new, unrecognizable athlete.

He realizes he needs to improve his rebounding. Having researched the rebounding skills and strategies of such individuals as Bill Russell, Dennis Rodman, and former N.Y. Knicks forward Sydney Green, Willis comes to understand that a large part of rebounding has to do with positioning, once the ball is in the air. Unfortunately, he does not possess a naturally instinctual feel for positioning near the basket once the ball has begun its trajectory. No matter. He will learn to emulate the instinctive rebounding moves of the great centers and forwards of the past. What is engraved foremost in Willis's mind is the idea that he will religiously train his legs and core in such a manner as to astound onlookers when the upcoming season begins. This should be the work ethic of any aspiring-to-be-great athlete during the off-season. Willis is aflame with the idea that "pretty good" will no longer be the way others describe him.

How does fierce desire actually translate into material results? First, Willis asks an assistant coach to help determine the exact height of his vertical leap, and he records the result in his athlete's notebook. Second, following extensive research, he devises a master plan intended to transform himself into a star attraction. He has noticed that during the "official" off-season practices and gym workouts, there is more talking, sitting, and kidding than there is sustained, hard work. He ignores the individuals who are just going through the motions and concentrates on doing what he is told to do. In addition, Willis has determined that the best way to improve radically is to undertake a regimen of core and plyometrically calibrated exercises on his own. He has obtained special permission to complement the normal routine workouts with his own regimen that consists of core weight work (squat press, deadlift, bench press, etc.), frog leaps, steep-hill-running, and box jumps (the latter with the help of two spotters).

When he has the time, Willis joins a Hatha yoga class or plays handball at a local fitness club. He finds that the latter sport positively affects his reflexes.

Little by little, using imagination and good sense, Willis continues to add to the strategic training mix. For one, he carries a basketball with him at all times during the off-season. Whenever the chance presents itself he practices dribbling, much like his idol Oscar Robertson did during his playing days at the University of Cincinnati. He is not embarrassed to practice anywhere appropriate, even as people watch. He also practices ball control by dribbling with his eyes looking upwards, and becomes familiar shooting from every possible angle and position on the court. Hours a day are sometimes spent on the foul line as well as working on his three-point shot. Only soreness in the arm and shoulder stops him from continuing. By the time the next season rolls around, Willis is ready to show the world what steady, innovative training in the off-season has produced: a jumping phenomenon who can also shoot and dribble skillfully.

His off-season strategy pays off. "Willis who?" the fans used to ask. Now he is referred to as an All-American.

Up to now the authors of this book have insisted on the necessity of following your training schedule assiduously. You might protest that Willis plays handball and takes yoga classes when he has the time. Moreover, on occasion, he even swims laps. Allow us to clear up the confusion. Ideally, the training blueprint is sacred. It should be followed religiously. However, it should include rest days and reflect the principle of *periodization*; that is, it should change the innovative workout strategies every twelve weeks. Thus, the blueprint avoids the effects of too much training of the same kind, creating adaptation issues.

## KEY TAKEAWAYS

- Implementing a strong work ethic and sticking to a well-thought-out workout plan can be more easily achieved with the help of mind control techniques.
- Devise your daily off-season workout/rest agenda with input from coaches, professional trainers, and specialized magazines, books,

and trustworthy websites. If you can attend an instructive seminar, do so.

- The nature of your workout ethic is affected by your general day-to-day conduct and values. Self-discipline and diligence with regard to nutrition, sleep, choosing friends, and avoiding trouble are essential. More about this later.

- The off-season is a time for transformation. You should be burning with a desire to improve to the extent that you shock your coaches and teammates when pre-season or early collective training begins.

- Off-season training agendas should incorporate elements that are meant to eliminate physical and skill-related weaknesses so you can "raise the bar" in your chosen sport.

- Try to devise workout strategies that are innovative and effective. The workout blueprint should reflect the concept of *periodization.*

# 6

# Setting Goals and Creating a Workout Blueprint

*A goal is a dream with a deadline.*

—Napoleon Hill

**YVONNE GOOLAGONG GREW UP**
in Barellan, New South Wales, Australia. Her identity and fate could easily have been sealed at birth by the fact that she was born into a large aborigine family, part of the Wiradjuri people. The indigenous Aboriginal Australian race had been historically subject, like the American Indians, to brutal prejudice and oppression at the hands of dominant waves of immigrants. However, Goolagong was born with a serene nature that was not adversely affected by growing up in the non-aborigine town of Barellan. As a pre-adolescent, she spent long hours hitting tennis balls against a cement wall, developing a wicked backhand that time and coaching never altered.

Often, she would wander over to the local tennis club and peer through the fence at members playing on clay courts. On one of these occasions, someone invited her into the club and encouraged her to pursue her tennis dreams as a guest member. In time, another club member, Vic Edwards, entered her life. He not only coached her, but took pains to ensure she evolved into a well-educated, well-spoken, poised individual. Goolagong began to work tirelessly to improve her tennis game. In the 1970s, she achieved most of her goals, winning seven

Grand Slam singles titles and reaching eighteen Grand Slam finals. This was quite a record for the athletic, well-coordinated youngster who not only had a dream but possessed the self-discipline and steadfast courage necessary to partly dominate women's tennis for over a decade.

Goolagong's example shows that athletes who set specific, measurable goals are well on their way to achieving them. In this chapter, we'll talk about what it takes to set, record, and follow through on your goals. We'll also offer up a sample workout blueprint so you can see how detailed and precise it is with regard to diet and exercise, then discuss the importance of innovation and trying new things in your training.

## Objective Goals and the SMART Philosophy

To set goals and determine the best action plan for success, you need to be smart. This means setting "objective" goals that relate specifically to your desired athletic performance. For example, the objective goal of lowering your time by a second in the 50-meter freestyle swim event is focused on what needs to be done physically and mentally to achieve it. Having a specific objective goal then helps you be more focused on incorporating new technical and tactical strategies that in turn lead to improved performance.

Let us look at a specific example of this kind of goal-setting. Back in 1962, a young man named James F. "Sandy" Van Kennen, Jr. entered Wesleyan University in Connecticut. He had been an All-American high school swimmer, and his goal in college was to compete successfully against the best college swimmers in the 50- and 100-yard swims. He decided that part of his goal-attainment strategy would be to swim long distances in the early morning and to do one hour of free-weight and elastic cord-pull exercises in the weight room before going downstairs to join his teammates at the main daily afternoon practice. He was alone in the small, cramped weight room. Van Kennen never missed a planned weight room session. In the pool, he always executed the coach's selected workout just like anyone else on the Wesleyan team, even though he had already completed some strenuous training on his own.

In the early spring of 1966 Van Kennen was invited, based on his swim times, to participate in the NCAA National Indoor Short Course Swim Championships.

His ultimate goal was in sight: win the 50-yard sprint despite coming from a school in the deep shadows of powerhouses such as Yale and Indiana University. Van Kennen swam well through the heats and awaited the finals of the 50-yard swim. As we have stated many times elsewhere, the elite athlete always remains focused and observant. During the heats, he noticed that in the short-course 25-yard pool, the participants in the 50-yard swim created a wave in their wake as they sprinted the first twenty-five yards. As they completed their flip turn and pushed off the wall to resume their stroke they "hit" the wave they had created on the first half of their swim. Van Kennen decided that immediately following his flip turn in the finals he would stay underwater, while kicking, for one additional second in order to allow the wave to pass overhead. The 1966 NCAA Division I National Short Course 50-yard champion was Sandy Van Kennen. All the years of hard work, early-morning long swims, and extra weight room practices paid off, as did his careful observation of his competitors at the meet. The goal Van Kennen had visualized for so many years was achieved against great odds.

There is an art to setting goals. One popular method athletes and coaches use is known as "SMART" goals:

- S-Set Specific goals: Your goals must be spelled out in clear detail. Vague goals are not attainable because they do not provide sufficient direction. "I will be the best golfer I can be" is not as specific as "I will finish in the top three as a sophomore in the Brighton Links tournament." Remember, you need specific goals to show you the way; goals should be palpable and easily visualized.

- M-Set Measurable goals: A measurable goal is one that can be tracked in numbers or amounts, like "by August 15 I will improve my baseball batting average to .350," or "by our first game I will have improved my basketball free throw shooting average by 20 percent." In this manner you can identify exactly how close you came to completing every phase of the master plan. Total or near-total success can be celebrated.

- A-Set Attainable goals: Take care to create goals that are realistic, not ones that are way too difficult to achieve. Keep in mind that you are setting goals for yourself, not your whole team—you can't always control whether the team wins or loses. Any goals you set need to be attainable by you as an individual. When setting goals, be sure to pick ones that are realistic but nonetheless hard to reach. You want to be challenged, but you do not want to set yourself up for failure or discouragement.

- **R**-Set Relevant goals: Goals should reflect the vision you have of your near and long-term future. What direction do you want to take in your sport—and in your life?

- T-Set Time: Part of the successful completion of the goal-attaining process hinges on time limits. These will enhance the chances that you will stick to the master plan.

In your objective goal-setting you are going to want to set at least one short-term and one long-term goal. Examples of short-term goals could be:

- During the fall season, I am determined to sleep eight hours a night.
- Each of my next six-mile practice runs will be over hilly terrain.

For your short-term goals, you want to focus on what you can achieve this season, and possibly even this week. You may have one or several, though you don't want so many goals at one time that you overextend yourself. The key is to make sure they are specific and actionable.

You will also want some objective long-term goals, reflecting your ultimate dreams in your sport. Long-term goals have you thinking past the immediate competition or season to what you want to happen next year or even a few years down the road. Some long-term goals might be:

- "By the beginning of the 2017 football season, I would like to become a starter and to avoid injuries by following a special warmup and flexibility regimen."

- "By next year I will experience a full recovery of my knee and shoulder injuries by faithfully attending my prescribed rehabilitation sessions and successfully dealing with the discomfort I may experience there."

## Recording and Following through with Your Goals

Once you have defined your goals in detail, write them down. Tell your friends about your plans so they can hold you accountable. Consider obtaining a dry-eraser board and easel on which to copy day-to-day goals, or using a mobile app like GoalsOnTrack to help you record your goal and track your daily progress. In this manner, you "see" and internalize the next day's training particulars before going to bed and upon waking.

Consider breaking down your overall plan into sixty- or ninety-day segments. This approach may help you remain focused. Every sixty or ninety days you will be rewarded for having successfully met the intermediary challenge. Set new or adjusted goals every sixty or ninety days. The ones you have not managed to reach during the off-season, despite your best efforts, are moved to the following sixty- to ninety-day blueprint. It may be that several years elapse before your ultimate goals are reached. However, the goals that take a long time to attain often provide the greatest satisfaction, for they represent an end point attained through long-term conviction and persistence. The sixty- or ninety-day time period mentioned above reflects the *periodization* strategy alluded to above. Moreover, within a *periodization* segment, training methods should be varied to avoid muscle adaptation and staleness.

Whatever detailed goals you set should be retained electronically and also be written down in a separate training notebook. You'll want to keep this with you at all times so you can refer to it regularly and take the time to visualize your next workout. The training plan is the day-to-day map of how you intend to achieve the short-term and long-term goals you have set for yourself. Having written down the detailed structure of each workout helps ensure the likelihood of completing it.

Having a well-thought-out and effective training plan helps you avoid monotonous aspects of training that lead to discouragement and overtraining.

At regular intervals, you can bathe in the satisfaction of having worked your way through X number of arduous but varied and invigorating training sessions. This knowledge is critical in solidifying a confident outlook not only during the competitive season but also in the off-season, which is when the highly-motivated athlete should consult successful coaches and expert trainers to supplement information readily available in magazines, books, and online. Whatever approach you take to structuring a training road map, be sure to choose a mix of strategies that coincide with your particular needs and workout style preferences. For example, it may be that a combination of CrossFit, plyometric, interval, and sand-box exercises appeals to you, while spin class and gym machine-training are less motivating.

You may find that when you are translating your goals into an overall training plan, a few inevitable distortions appear. Your blueprint may be charged with too many details or it may turn out to be too general. Also, the blueprint is sometimes so ambitious that there is not enough time to undertake all its dimensions or to get enough restorative sleep. When the latter is the case, it is often necessary to modify the plan as it evolves. Flexibility is key, especially when you are new to setting athletic goals and creating workout scenarios. You want to stay true to your goals, but understand that with practice you will get better at setting realistic goals and deadlines.

## A Sample Blueprint

Let us, as an example, map out a concrete, comprehensive off-season workout plan for a middle-distance runner named Paul. This detailed road map will make the paragraphs and chapters that follow more illuminating, since it deals with specific exercises and foods that are helpful for aspiring athletes.

First of all, Paul checks his equipment, particularly his running shoes, and makes the appropriate purchases. Next, Paul writes out breakfast, lunch, and dinner menus for a typical two-week period. While we will address nutrition more fully in chapter 10, for now be aware that the key meal items are the following:

Breakfast: Healthy options include granola, Swiss muesli, bran oats, goat-milk yogurt, long-grain brown rice (basmati), eggs (two to four a week), strawberries, apples, walnuts, almonds, freshly-squeezed orange juice, coconut water, beet juice, pomegranate juice, coffee/chicory mix, ginseng tea, and whole grain toast. The long-grain brown rice needs to be chewed well. Once cooked (usually approximately one hour), it can be stored in the refrigerator for quite a few days. For individuals who enjoy smoothies for breakfast, a healthy mix can include varied-color berries, apple, kiwi, peach, kale, almonds, almond milk, and three ice cubes. Any fruit should be rinsed.

Lunch: Some excellent choices are salmon, tuna, shrimp, chicken, turkey, angel hair spaghetti with a moderate portion of grated cheese, carrots, broccoli, Brussels sprouts, long-grain brown rice (basmati), asparagus, and salad with olive oil. Do not have soda or dessert (except fresh fruit). With any combination of the above, add fresh, washed celery stalks to improve digestion.

Dinner: The evening meal should be lighter than lunch. Good choices include salmon, scallops, sole, cod, chicken, turkey, long-grain brown rice (basmati), pasta with moderate amounts of grated cheese, a choice of dark vegetables, salad with olive oil, and apple.

Next, Paul sets his cell phone alarm for 10 p.m., to remind him of his bedtime, and 6:30 a.m. to alert him as to when it's time to wake up.

In the first weeks of November Paul runs approximately twenty aerobic miles per week. In addition, he goes to the gym most days to stretch and do yoga. Two days a week, following yoga class, Paul works out his upper and lower body using free weights and stationary machines. Beginning in the fourth week of November he adds fifteen miles of easy running, meaning that he is now running thirty-five miles per week. During the month of December Paul goes to the gym twice weekly to complete the following cardio (CrossFit/plyometric/core) workout:

- Warmup (light running in place, jumping jacks, stationary bike, and the like) followed by stretching;

- Three sets of 25-yard frog leaps;

- One set of twenty burpees;

- One set of fifteen burpees with a ten-pound weight in each hand;

- Two sets of ten medium-height box jumps (using two spotters in case of a fall);

- Four sets of 25-yard one-legged hops (alternate left and right leg);

- Two sets of 15-second high-knee rapid running in place;

- Abdominals;

- Cool down.

During December Paul is ready to follow the day-by-day recommendations of Arthur Lydiard drawn from his book, *Running to the Top:*

- Monday: Hill running for thirty to sixty minutes.

- Tuesday: High knee lift/long striding exercises.

- Wednesday: Hill running for thirty to sixty minutes.

- Thursday: Leg speed: one hundred meters by six to ten times.

- Friday: Relaxed striding two hundred meters by six times.

- Saturday: Hill running for thirty to sixty minutes.

- Sunday: Jogging for ninety minutes or more.

In January and February Paul continues following Lydiard's advice, adding to the intensity of his workouts:

- Monday: Repetition of eight hundred meters by six times or sixteen hundred meters by three times.

- Tuesday: Easy fartlek running for forty-five to sixty minutes.

- Wednesday: Repetition of eight hundred meters by six times or sixteen hundred meters by three times.

- Thursday: Fast relaxed running one hundred meters by ten times.

- Friday: Jogging for thirty minutes.

- Saturday: Repetitions of six hundred meters by six times or a thousand meters by four times.

- Sunday: Jogging for ninety minutes or more.

In March and April Paul mixes elements from above with fast relaxed running, windsprints (twelve to sixteen times), interval training, and time trials (two hundred to fifteen hundred meters). Hill running and twice-weekly gym work are part of the overall training strategy.

Paul's sample workout blueprint represents only one option among many. For instance, 800-meter world and Olympic champion, David Rudisha of Kenya, runs approximately sixty miles a week. Rudisha integrates long-distance running with tempo runs and fast intervals. In the final analysis, your coach and you will no doubt devise your own version of such regimens.

## Leveraging Your Workout Blueprint for Intensity and Endurance

In our system there exists no such thing as taking it easy except on your scheduled rest or light workout days. Regardless of your sport, if you assiduously follow the preseason training plan, the regular season will seem relatively easy by comparison. In principle, workouts need to be harder than what you will experience in regular-season practice and in competition. In addition, with the help of self-talk, the body will be able to handle fatigue in the last quarter or last part of competitions. If you are tired near the end of a competition, positive self-talk can produce a charge of energy that allows the body to function at its highest level till time runs out.

As you set goals and plan your workout blueprint, it's important to think about your level of training intensity. It should be stated that our emphasis on "rigorous" and "all-out" workouts in the off-season does not necessarily apply to all athletes, all of the time. For example, certain middle-and-long-distance runners regularly favor volume rather than intensity for well-thought-out strategic reasons. However, for 400-meter standouts who follow the training philosophy of Baylor University's coach, Clyde Hart, short but intense workouts are often the rule. Essentially, the overall training plan should reflect innovative, well-thought-out principles that aim at raising the bar without incurring injury. Of course, in the majority of sports—swimming, wrestling, football, skiing, speed skating, gymnastics, and so on—rigorous, out-of-breath workouts are the rule.

A word on obstacle course racing is appropriate here. A serious distance track athlete can profit handsomely from participating in obstacle course racing such as Spartan Race, Tough Mudder, or Warrior dash, particularly when the event is a long-distance one. The American Olympic wrestler, Jordan Burroughs, has profited from such training.

You will also want to follow a workout road map that increases your overall endurance. In modern dictionaries, one of the connotations of the word "endurance" is the ability to withstand pain. If you are training or are intent on training for a marathon or a full triathlon—even a half-marathon or Olympic-length triathlon—your training will no doubt produce some measure of pain. It is quite interesting to notice how impressed people are when they meet someone who has participated in and finished a long-distance athletic event. The truth is that, if trained for properly, the hard part of distance events is not necessarily the competition itself—unless you are a professional or are looking to better your personal record (PR)—but rather the training prior to the competition.

A good example of unwavering endurance is embodied in the work ethic of the German national soccer team. Take a look at one of their matches: Notice how in the last minutes of a grueling encounter, the players are running up and down the field with the same speed and concentrated explosiveness as they were at the very beginning of the match. This is why the German team is perennially ranked in the top three in the world, and why they won the 2014 World Cup. They simply will not slow down or give up.

Today, ultra-running has captured the imagination of many runners as evidenced by the plethora of magazines devoted to this ultra-endurance sport. Ultra-running events now number in the vicinity of 1,200 per year. However, regularly training for and participating in 100-mile-plus competitions puts a strain on the heart. Micah True of ultra-running fame was in the habit of running a hundred miles or so on training days. An enlarged heart killed him on one of his shorter training runs. Numerous research studies indicate that as ultra-endurance runners age they may encounter a host of serious disabilities, including the need for a pacemaker implant. Those individuals (men and women) who are ultra-runners should have a cardiac stress test done once a year.

With regard to training, in general, keep the following points in mind. Try to develop a burning passion for working out. Be humble in that you recognize the need to work on weaknesses. Even the great tennis champion, Rafael Nadal, in the early stages of his maturity, did not serve with power and fluidity. It took years of practice and repetition to get it right. While perfectionism can be a sign of mental imperfection, when applied to training, it represents an advantage. When working out, keep in mind that perfect form equals the most natural, efficacious movement the athlete can produce. Lastly, vary the type of daily workout and the muscle group(s) affected.

The closer you come to sticking to your workout blueprint in all its particulars, provided that your overall plan is well-thought-out and rigorous, the more your endurance will increase and the more confident you will be when competition begins. How exactly is this the case? Well, imagine that you are a wrestler or a long-distance runner, or any other type of athlete who is subject to exhaustion. When you feel like giving up, you can recall that you never, or nearly never, compromised during your arduous training sessions. In the just cited situation, you can start to repeat the following mantra: "If I am hurting; then my adversaries are hurting a lot more."

## Innovative Training: Enhance Your Workout Strategy

As you set goals and create your workout blueprint, you will need to remain open to innovation. When we encourage innovative modes of working out, we are not at all recommending the invention of exercises that turn out to be dangerous and cause injury. Rather, we want you to use your imagination to tap into novel but effective ways of reaching tour-de-force performances in your sports field.

Nino Benvenuti, world middleweight boxing champion (1968–1970), trained for upcoming fights in both a traditional and unconventional manner. Though he worked on the speed bag on a regular basis, he also set up a series of floor-to-ceiling rubber cords with a speed bag type of ball attached to the cord about head high that his trainer would pull at varied angles and with varied tension. Benvenuti would then punch the ball, which was moving at great speed and in unpredictable trajectories. Benvenuti also had trainers throw different types of inflated balls at him in a type of one-man dodge ball to sharpen his reflexes. It was Benvenuti's innovative approach to training that translated into defensive and offensive moves that tended to befuddle his opponents. It is interesting to note how few modern boxers have, beyond the standard approaches to training, imitated Benvenuti's innovative ways.

When training guide-books speak about the ideal qualitites of an elite athlete, they regularly mention stamina, strength, flexibility, power, speed, coordination, and agility. To these attributes, *reflexes* should be added. Without belaboring the point, let it be said that football backs, soccer players, and others, need sharp reflexes to perform effectively.

Creativity in his training methods helped Javier Sotomayor, standing at 6' 5" and weighing 181 pounds, become not only the greatest high jumper of the modern era, but also the best high jumper of all time. The legendary Cuban has held the world high-jump record (eight feet and a quarter inch) for the past twenty-eight years. He is a four-time world and two-time Olympic champion. Sotomayor's innovative training methods are responsible for his long-term dominance of a succession of worthy rivals. Early in his career Sotomayor combined core work with stadium step climbs and frog leaps on sandy terrain. The last mentioned evolved into single-leg bounding on the same surface. At times, during gym workouts, Sotomayor wore a ninety-pound vest. As regards core work, he eventually increased his squat-lift weight to six hundred pounds. We also know that Sotomayor spent time running, hopping, and jumping in a specially designed swimming pool. Innovative training means that you will remain open to techniques drawn from diverse sources. In their unique book *Free+Style* (2014), Carl Paoli and Anthony Sherbondy explore ways to complement and maximize sport-specific training with experiences across multiple disciplines. They believe that high-performing athletes need to experience basic movement patterns that are foreign to their specific sport (as did Michael Jordan) in order to make significant advances in their own sport. To follow this example, it is vital to bypass conventional wisdom and seek out original ways through CrossFit workouts to enhance improvement in your own field of endeavor. Here again we are touching on the importance of taking independent, original, imaginative initiatives to raise your individual mastery level in your own sport. Don't allow other people's thinking to thwart your own new approaches to skill acquisition. Carl Paoli, originally a gymnast, says he "made the biggest leap by far" in his thinking when he began studying CrossFit, which he calls "fitness for elite athletes." CrossFit, he explains, "is the culmination of an enormous experiment on how the human body can address various challenges and which adaptations are the most successful at helping people move better."

Another illustration of the importance of innovation involves an imaginary professional pitcher, Frank. He has endured several mediocre seasons and is now home between campaigns. There, Frank runs into a physical therapist. Following a long conversation centered on a strategic regimen the therapist has in mind, designed to change the pitcher's fortunes, Frank begins daily early-morning workouts in the basement of the physical therapist's home. The therapist loves the game of baseball and has, for a number of years now, desired to apply his personal theories related to how to improve a pitcher's effectiveness on the mound. In short order, Frank feels transformed. He has lost some weight and has completely changed his eating habits for the better. What has already intrigued Frank the most, however, is the substance of his daily workouts, a combination of stretching, mobility drills, core work, and varied pulley-apparatus exercises. Following each session in the basement, Frank and his now trusted friend, the therapist, move to the backyard where the therapist has Frank pitch to him at half-speed, but in a full windup. Frank, following the therapist's instructions, is raising his lead leg higher and is reaching back with the baseball in a more extended manner.

In time, always following a warm-up and flexibility routine, the therapist has Frank throwing full-speed fastballs as well as a variety of other pitches (curve, slider, change-up, etc.) at a moving target within the strike zone. In time, Frank radically improves his placement of pitches while also getting the baseball to dart or move at the last second. Frank is a new man and moves his body with the fluidity and agility of a hip-hop dancer on the mound. His pitching motion, particularly its final phase, now resembles a whiplash phenomenon. Frank's teammates and coaches can hardly recognize him during spring training, and during the season he goes on to win twenty-one games against seven losses. He is perceived by the media as a more accurate, more durable, second coming of former New York Yankee fireballer, Ryne Duren.

If this story sounds unrealistic, consult the 2014 *Sports Illustrated* article on the L.A. Dodgers pitcher, Clayton Kershaw. Though 6' 4" tall and carrying 225 pounds, Kershaw did not attain true effectiveness on the mound until he signed up for sixteen clinic sessions with Navarro College head coach Skip Johnson. The *S.I.* author, Lee Jenkins, put it this way:

> In 2005, Kershaw was not the Ideal Pitcher. The high school junior threw from a three-quarter arm slot, didn't deploy his lower body and barely cracked 90 miles per hour. That fall he signed up for 16 sessions spanning two months with Navarro College head coach Skip Johnson, and together they reshaped his mechanics at a Dallas baseball academy. Kershaw raised his release point. He lengthened his stride. He kept his weight back, turning his body into a bow, as [Sandy] Koufax likes to say. "He got that fast-twitch explosion," explains Johnson . . . . Scouts started clocking him at 94–96 mph.

Incidentally, Kershaw went 21-3 with a 1.77 ERA in the 2014 season for the L.A. Dodgers. Clearly, a change in throwing mechanics plus core-and-flexibility work made all the difference—as did Kershaw's willingness to incorporate novel methods into his workouts, ones that no one else was practicing.

Before concluding this chapter, let us list some of the innovative CrossFit, plyometric, and cardio exercises in vogue today.

- Sand-dune running

- Sand-box or beach-sand hopping (one leg or two)

- Rope climbing

- Sand-bag manipulation

- Medicine ball slamming or throwing (forward or backward)

- Single-leg dead lift/single-leg squats

- Spinning class (stationary bike)

- Barre class (flexibility)

- Sled push or pull

- Two-legged or single-leg box jumping (with two spotters)

- Two-legged lateral jumps (with two spotters)

- Battling ropes

- Ladder training

- Chin-ups with a weighted vest

- Kettlebell movements

- Timed agility runs (using cones)

- Locomotive drill with a sudden change of direction

- Loaded movement training

- Skipping rope (with good form)

- Ab-roller from kneeling position

- Yoga and Pilates

Let us repeat: When we encourage innovative workout modes, we are not at all recommending the invention of exercises that turn out to be dangerous and cause injury. Rather, we are speaking of using your imagination to tap into novel but effective ways of reaching tour-de-force performances in your sports field. Herb Elliott, undefeated in the mile and 1,500 meters between 1957 and 1961,

# Cardio/Plyometrics/ Cross/Fit

attributes his success to novel training methods: for example, repeatedly running up steep sand dunes in Portsea, Australia.

In conclusion, the athlete who wants to achieve or maintain elite sport status should be a self-disciplined individual. Part of that discipline entails writing down in detail the workout and rest regimen best suited to achieve the ultimate goal. The off-season training plan can be modified along the way, but should not be compromised to any significant extent. Of course, particularly at the college and pro levels, professional trainers and coaches often devise the workout regimen. However, as we shall see later, this does not preclude your input based on your unique experience, needs and research.

## KEY TAKEAWAYS

- Elite athletes need to set goals that fit the SMART model: the goals are specific, measureable, attainable, relevant, and timely.

- You will want to set both short-term and long-term athletic goals for yourself.

- Utilize a detailed workout training plan. Be careful not to derail your progress due to unhealthy eating, emotional upset, lack of sleep, late-night socializing, or overtraining.

- The elite athlete trains harder and in a more intelligent, creative manner than any potential opponent. Workouts need to be harder than what you will experience during pre- and regular-season practice and in competition.

- Strive to imagine and incorporate safe, innovative training methods into your workout blueprint.

# 7

# Preparing for the Workout

*I believe that the conscious presence in each moment is the golden key to effective practice. Practice is not going through the motions with our body while our mind and spirit reside elsewhere. Rather, practice is about focused effort with our entire being. This engrains habit and skill into our unconscious self.*

—Jim Afremow

**TYLER VARGA'S UNWAVERING DETERMINATION** sets him apart from other college football players. At 5' 11" and 225 pounds, the Yale running back does not distinguish himself purely on brute force. According to the *New York Times*, the primary reason Varga is so "unstoppable" is his workout habits—habits that lead even his own teammates to sometimes look at him as though he has lost his mind. He adheres to a "meticulous diet" that includes rice and egg whites and a schedule that requires him to wake up every two hours to eat. After the team does its lifting together in the varsity gym, Varga goes off by himself to lift some more in the recreational gym. His tremendous effort has paid off: during his first season at Yale, he led the country in all-purpose yards per game and for the most rushing yards in the Ivy League.

If you are serious about being an elite athlete or reaching your full potential, don't just do what the others are doing; instead, be like Tyler Varga. Gain an advantage over your opponents by working harder than they do. The athletes who succeed are the ones who go the extra mile—often literally. This begins by preparing the body and mind for rigorous workouts. Each time you hit the gym, strive to obtain the full value of the workout. We use the word "value" because without optimum workouts, you cannot get stronger, faster, or better. A lot of athletes experience two or maybe three good workouts a week. The other two or three amount to going through the motions. How you react to a hot or cold climate, to wake-up fatigue, late afternoon blues, and so on can constitute the difference between successful and mediocre training.

## Preparing Physically for Your Workouts

How can you prepare your mind and body properly for each workout? There are several essential things that you need to do in order for your body to be in peak form for each training session. Because you will be training often and intensely, these habits have to become a part of your daily life, as regular as breathing. You can't just trot them out when it's convenient for you and then abandon them when you get stressed or your routine is disrupted because you're traveling or have an exam coming up.

*Sleep.* Be sure your body is rested. You cannot stay up late and expect to perform well. Make getting the rest you need a priority. Sleep the appropriate number of hours, usually in the range of seven to ten. If you regularly forgo sleep, the consequences can be severe for your training and your health. Ellington Darden in his book *The New High Intensity Training* warns that lack of sleep for several nights "increases brain levels of cortisol, a potentially dangerous stress hormone." This can result in a weakened immune system which, in turn, may lead to depression, irritability, low energy, and a lower pain threshold. One recent study on sleep demonstrated that adults who only got five to six hours of sleep a night were four times more likely than those who slept seven or more hours to become sick when exposed to a virus. People who don't get enough sleep are, over time, at increased risk of gaining weight, suffering from coronary artery disease and, in the long run, being subject to forms of dementia such as Alzheimer's.

Remember, too, that scientists' recommendation that adults sleep at least seven and teenagers nine hours a night is *for ordinary people during ordinary times,* not for elite or ambitious athletes who are pushing their bodies to accomplish far more than the average person. Research shows that athletes perform better when they're at the high end of a seven-to-ten hour range. For example, an ongoing study at Stanford University has tracked the effect of additional sleep on Stanford's varsity athletes. The findings? When sleeping a full ten hours a night, Stanford's tennis players improved their quickness on the court and the accuracy of their shots. Its swimmers and basketball players likewise performed better and reported more upbeat moods when they got the optimal ten hours of sleep a night. Sleep is important for your athletic success not just because you are warding off illness and fatigue, but because nighttime is when your body releases hormones that stimulate your muscles to grow and to repair themselves. Sleep is vital to your training. Don't skimp on it.

If you are striving to become self-disciplined on your way to achieving elite status in your sport, take care to maintain good sleep habits such as going to bed at the same time each evening and rising at the same time each morning. This is not as easy as it sounds: it entails skipping late-night eating and outings with your friends. Road trips to major cities are especially enticing, each sporting a rich variety of late-night activity. To help ensure your ability to forgo the party scene, let your friends know that you have begun a new health regimen that requires you to get a good night's sleep every night.

To help ensure that your sleep is restful, place your bed as far from windows as you can. Turn the thermostat down to 65 degrees. If you are able, invest in double-paned windows, which muffle outside noises. The room in which you sleep should be as dark and silent as possible. This means no ticking alarm clocks, glowing cell phone screens, or blinking computer lights. Pack your gym bag the night before with everything you need for your workout, so you won't have to worry about it in the morning. Make sure you make your bed each morning after having rolled down the sheet and covers to let the bed breathe. Periodically, turn the mattress over while placing the head at the foot of the bed. Change the sheets and pillowcases regularly. Try to vacuum your living space twice weekly to breathe more efficiently. Try not to drink or eat in the hours preceding bedtime, unless you require something like a chamomile herbal tea to help you sleep. Sound, sufficient sleep will ensure that the mind is functioning clearly from the moment you wake up. Assuming that your nutritional habits and psychological state of mind are in order, you will thus be looking forward with enthusiasm to fulfilling your day's training schedule.

*Eat right.* As an athlete, you will want to learn which foods provide you with superior energy. When you experience a great workout, write down what you ate, the time you ate it prior to your workout, how much sleep you had, and how much fluid you imbibed before the workout. Do the same as regards the food and drink you consume after the workout.

This careful record-keeping will help you learn a truth that elite athletes know: Not all foods are created equal.

"We are what we eat." This little bit of wisdom holds ramifications that touch on the quality of workouts. Food choices can make a critical difference at workout time. If you eat a heavy meal marked principally by saturated fat at a fast-food establishment before your workout, you will feel sluggish when it is time to perform. The same will occur if you are prone to eating large desserts. Instead, two or three hours before the workout, you want to eat something that helps you feel light and ready to go instead of heavy and fatigued. Moreover, consider a glass of beet juice before a heavy training session. Or, you can also mix it into a shake. A Kansas State University study found that beet juice has a highly beneficial effect on fast-twitch muscle fibers. It helps to widen your blood vessels, contributing to an improved distribution of nutrients and oxygen throughout your body.

For more tips on eating and nutrition, see chapter 10.

*See your doctor.* Before embarking on a strenuous workout regimen, remember to visit your health-care provider to check on your pulse rate, blood pressure, lung/breath capacity, and other standard measures. Although the tests may be expensive, you may also wish to undergo an electrocardiogram (ECG), and an echocardiogram. The latter uses sound waves to monitor the heart, and is considered "the best test for diagnosing structural heart disorders, such as aortic-valve-enlargements [and] hypertrophic cardiomyopathy." Finally, you might undergo a cardiac stress test, where you are hooked up to an ECG and a blood-pressure monitor while exercising on a treadmill. A stress test allows doctors to examine how well your heart is functioning and whether you may have any arterial blockage.

You can do preventive maintenance to keep the body from breaking down: warm up and stretch before and after the workout; treat inflamed areas or injuries to joints or tendons with ice (twenty minutes maximum); and take advantage of body massages, if your athletic program offers them.

## Choose the Right Workout Environment

Regardless of the school or professional team/club you belong to, you may find yourself working out at a training center during the off-season. It is crucial that the most appropriate center and trainer be chosen. The interplay of trainers, atmosphere, and equipment must be such that they emotionally motivate you to believe you are going to rise to the next level. Whether it is the young swim phenom who wakes up at 5:00 a.m. to join a group of swimmers at an aquatic center to train under the guidance of a world-class coach, or a highly rated equestrian compound whose members groom their respective horses at dawn before putting them through their paces under the watchful eye of the trainer, the underlying motivational incentive is the same. Now that you have found what you consider to be the best available training environment, go all-out to raise the bar in your quest for athletic excellence.

## Preparing Mentally for Your Workouts

Mental and emotional preparation is crucial to fruitful training. Likely, there will be days when you don't feel like working out. Keep these to a minimum with proper sleep and eating habits. Remember, if your mind is not totally committed, you will not be able to give 100 percent to your training that day.

*Commit to giving it your all.* If you work out five times per week, you should work out to the maximum capacity. Few athletes do this, but the ones who do are the elite performers.

Train the brain so that you do not lose focus while working out. While others are talking, joking, laughing, or going through the motions, you are concentrated on the tasks at hand. Try to become familiar with pain; remember that a burning sensation is usually a sign of progress. Lastly, as we have mentioned earlier, base your workout agenda on the most up-to-date information. Take the initiative to go to the bookstore and the library; go see coaches. If you are a professional and have the means, travel to seminars, conferences, and training centers. In any case, strive to absorb the latest methods and psychological approaches to cutting-edge training. One last point in the latter context: One often reads today that the adage, "no pain, no gain" represents a passé strategy. We beg to differ. Though it is true that, for example, aerobic runs may offer the best overall long-distance running strategy, we believe that if you don't mix in occasional relatively long tempo runs with fast, repeat 400s, 800s, or miles, you will not be fully prepared on race day.

*Remember your mental strategies.* All of the mind-control strategies we learned about at the beginning of the book can help you tremendously as you seek to get motivated for your workouts. This is where self-talk, textual recordings, auto-suggestion, and visualization come into play. Read your script or listen to your recording before bed, first thing in the morning, and before workouts. Visualize the perfect execution of elements that comprise the workout. By doing so, you will maintain a high level of motivation.

You also want to carefully study what your opponents are doing. Consider the example of Randy Couture, a bright individual who graduated from Oklahoma State with a 4.0 GPA. To prepare for upcoming fights, Randy watched all the videos of his opponents that he could lay his hands on. With the knowledge acquired through video study, he modified his workout routines to better counter his opponents' fighting style. For example, having observed that Vitor Belfort always begins to throw a flurry of punches with his left hand, Randy modified the boxing part of his workouts by circling left when his sparring partner moved in leading with a left-hand punch. Although many mixed martial arts pundits had predicted that Belfort would win handily, Couture came out the victor. Couture's analytical study of his opponents in preparation for battles that he was expected to lose have made all the difference.

Don't forget the visualization strategies we learned in Part I. Consider the example of Kasha, a competitive cheerleader whose specialty is tumbling and stunting. Before departing for a workout, Kasha sits in a living room armchair without opening the blinds and visualizes her upcoming training session. She mentally pictures every detail of her team's latest routine. She pictures herself as the center of attention in a huge, sold-out auditorium that is now silent, attention riveted on her team. She hears the opening bars of the music, then sees herself transported into perfected movements and postures. As the music score reaches crescendo-like heights, Kasha sees herself vaulting through the air, landing in superb fashion on steady legs. She hears the deafening roar of the crowd. She sees her mother shedding tears and her coach waiting with open arms for her. She sees her teammates happily descending from the stage once they have bowed to the judges.

*Stay positive.* Listening to your favorite music during the workout can be a positive motivating factor. However, on days when you feel pumped and ready to experience a strongly beneficial training session, leave the music at home or in your gym bag. This way you save the music for days when you are relatively more fatigued compared to your normal pre-workout state.

Workouts can be fun. For example, as Kasha and her teammates rehearse, she is wholly focused on both her individual role and its integration within the overall team's routine. Rather than exhibiting anxiety or fear, Kasha is lost in an instinctively sure-footed and sure-handed exhibition of her finely tuned talents. Kasha's cheerleading team repeats its number over and over until each tumble, jump, flip, stunt, and cheer meets the approval of the perfectionist team coach. Kasha thrives on such a demanding, time-consuming dance practice. If one were to ask what she thought of her workout, Kasha would no doubt respond by saying, "It was a lot of fun."

All of the strategies in this chapter, both physical and mental, aim to help you have effective workouts that move you to a higher level of achievement. Are you ready to stand out? Are you ready to feel light and explosive? Then prepare mentally and physically without letting anything or anyone impede your progress. Picture it, think it, repeat it, and do it!

## KEY TAKEAWAYS

- The evening before a morning workout, prepare your gym bag. Get a good night's sleep. Aim for a minimum of seven hours, with ten being the gold standard.

- Avoid consuming a fast-food meal before a workout. Unhealthy eating will likely result in a sluggish feeling and a less motivated state of mind.

- The evening before a morning workout, visualize the ideal training process and results. Do not compromise by changing the blueprint unless you are enhancing it with cutting-edge training procedures or modifying it based on sound reasoning.

- Try to make the workout exciting.

# 8

# Warming Up and Increasing Your Flexibility

*Increase flexibility in your muscle to become faster and stronger;*

*increase flexibility in your mind to become smarter; increase the size of*

*your heart to be more loving.*

—Master Hill

## THE TWO AUTHORS OF THIS BOOK

work out and train others at the same fitness center. Over our many years of experience we have been consistently surprised at how few individuals—star athletes included—bother to warm up and stretch before beginning their exercise routines. At the same time, many of these same individuals complain of physical problems usually related to the knee, back, hip, or shoulder. A number of our club members between the ages of forty and seventy have had one or more knee, back, or shoulder surgeries. We wonder how many of these medical interventions could have been avoided if those same individuals had made it a habit to warm up adequately, followed by stretching, before beginning their training sessions.

Elite athletes at all levels, regardless of their inherent flexibility, should make it a habit to initially warm up for ten minutes or more and then stretch all parts of the body before engaging in a strenuous workout. By the term "warm up" we mean one or several of the following movements: light running in place, moderate jump roping, jogging, executing jumping jacks, pedaling on a stationary bike, or just walking. Stretching follows the warm up phase. In this chapter, we'll take a look at the critical (and too often ignored) warmup and cool down, and also explore how improving your flexibility can help you perform better in your sport.

## Warming Up

Before your training session, allot plenty of time to warm up—at least ten minutes. You don't want to rush things here. Make sure to start the warm-up phase slowly and to wear running shoes that are not too worn out.

Professional trainers often tell their clients to warm up on a treadmill or elliptical trainer. Of the two, the latter would seem to be the better choice since the surface of treadmills can be relatively hard. If, for example, you are a serious runner who covers long weekly distances over ground that is softer than street or sidewalk surfaces, try to avoid running on a treadmill, particularly right before a competition. Working out on one can cause soreness in the calves.

The initial warmup phase should be followed by stretching. If you are not used to a certain progression of stretching movements or are not certain that these movements are adequate, consult any number of excellent books on the subject (see the bibliography at the end of this volume), including Robert A. Anderson's *Stretching* (2000). There are also several free YouTube videos based on Anderson's book if you would like to see how these stretches are safely performed. Basically, you want to stretch the hamstrings, the quads, the calves, and the abdominals (leaning the upper body backwards as you alternate arms reaching for the sky). The same approach applies to the upper body.

Once the warmup and stretching phases are complete, it is time to consult your training blueprint, if you have not already done so earlier in the day. The idea here is to ensure that you are fully aware of the prescribed particulars of the training session at hand. In this context, based on our own experience, it is better to leave your training manual at home and bring with you a copy of the sheet(s) corresponding to a particular workout. Why? Generally, because people tend, sooner or later, to forget the training manual at the gym, on the field, or at the pool, thereby risking the loss of an extremely valuable document. Moreover, it is best to save a copy to your computer. Of course, if your coach or trainer has mapped out the particulars of each training session, possessing your own copy of the planning blueprint is optional.

## Improving Flexibility

Stretching, after initially warming up, is absolutely essential to prevent injury. It is equally vital to stretch correctly; i.e., with correct form and only to a point that is comfortable. Naturally, retaining comfort when stretching also means not attempting to blindly "improve" on the previous day's stretching positions.

To illustrate the latter point in the context of pre-season football practice, let us briefly follow the experience of a tight end we will call Robert. Prior to arriving at pre-season football camp, Robert has worked out with friends at a vacation site on an Atlantic Ocean beach. These workouts have consisted of early morning running at the water's edge, playing touch football on the sand, and periodically exercising at a local gym. Stretching has been part of the equation. Upon arriving at camp, Robert feels loose and ready to go. However, the morning after the first two-a-day practice, he can hardly manage to get out of bed. It feels impossible for him to participate in the morning's workout. At breakfast, Robert notices that other players also show signs of stiffness and soreness. On the field that morning, Robert is unable to stretch nearly to the extent he was able to the day before. He resolves to stretch with care. In the sitting position, he leans over as best he can, enough to adequately stretch his hamstrings. He takes the same approach with other stretches he and his teammates execute after a ten-minute jog around the field. As the pre-season two-a-day workouts progress, Robert recovers his full range of leg and arm motion, but is careful to remain in his comfort zone, never overstretching.

If you are wondering why this book puts great emphasis on stretching, remember that without loose joints and musculature, explosive athletic performance is not easily and safely attained. To illustrate the point, imagine the difference between a broomstick and a rope. The broomstick cannot be manipulated easily and its configuration is one-dimensional. When enough pressure is applied to the broomstick, it breaks. The rope, on the other hand, can be configured into an infinite variety of positions and forms. Most important, the rope can be manipulated to move at great speed and with great force. The same can be said of the elite performer who is properly warmed up and flexible: he or she is able to produce quick, cobra-like movements without, in principle, incurring injury.

Yoga and Pilates are two techniques that can help you increase flexibility. Yoga is an Indian meditation and exercise technique that has been shown to reduce stress and anxiety. It is excellent for building better balance and flexibility. Find a group to practice with or take a class in a local gym, community center, or fitness club. As you have no doubt noticed, you can easily find a proliferation of yoga lessons online or on DVDs, which allow you to practice at home.

Pilates is a series of movements and body postures developed in Germany in the early twentieth century. With proper equipment and guidance, it can be very effective in improving strength, flexibility, and balance. Pilates works on the core, which is something we'll discuss in the next chapter; that is, it works the lower back, the buttocks, and the abdomen.

Despite the great potential benefits of yoga and Pilates, let it be said that they can also be dangerous. You should always avoid stretches that create strain or feel uncomfortable. Avoid certain difficult yoga poses such as standing on your head. In *The Science of Yoga: The Risks and the Rewards*, science journalist William J. Broad of the *New York Times* refers to a 2009 survey by a team from the Columbia College of Physicians and Surgeons, who asked therapists, yoga teachers, and doctors about the dangers of practicing yoga. Thirteen hundred individuals responded. The survey recorded the following injuries: lower back (231), shoulder (219), knee (174), neck (110), and stroke (4). The survey identified inadequate teacher training standards as the main reason for so many injuries. In the case of Pilates, given the types of stretches and movements it involves, it should also be practiced with care. Don't hesitate to skip poses that do not seem right for you. Just tell the yoga or Pilates master, if you need to, that you would rather not attempt this or that pose.

## Cooling Down

Let us assume that you have completed your workout and are ready to head home. Well, the fact of the matter is that your workout session is not over; the consensus of experts in the field of workout physiology is that a post-training-session "cool-down" is an often overlooked but essential element in the elite athlete's modus operandi. Laboratory clinical trials have proven beyond any doubt that ending a workout with a stretching session enhances the gains produced by the just-finished workout. Yes, we hear you: Some of our readers may be shaking their heads as they reason that a post-workout mini-stretching-session is too much. To those of you who are of such a mind, we address one question: Do you want to reach your full potential and attain elite athletic status or not? That is the crux of the matter. Superior performance entails sacrifices. Those of you who are ready and willing to do the right things will have the proverbial "edge" on the competition. The experts are all in agreement: A post-workout warm-down enhances the overall benefits of the training session.

## KEY TAKEAWAYS

- Important: At the beginning of a training session, warm up slowly for ten or more minutes *before* stretching.

- The initial warm-up phase of each workout may encompass one or more of the following: riding the stationary bike, jogging in place, jogging, elliptical training, jumping jacks, and jumping rope.

- If you feel unusual pain, a strain, or a pull, stop the workout immediately and ice down the injury. Make sure the injury is fully healed before returning to full-body workouts.

- Post-workout stretching is an essential part of the cool-down routine.

# Warm up

# Stretching

# 9

# Training the Core and Preventing Injury

*If you train hard, you'll not only be hard, you'll be hard to beat.*

—Herschel Walker

## WORK ETHIC, MIND CONTROL

(self-talk, auto-suggestion, visualization), and the right fuel for our bodies have now prepared us to train at extremely high levels. Ideally, the elite athlete trains harder and with a more intelligent strategy than any potential opponent. This strategy requires training the body to be extremely strong and in the case of contact sports, to withstand punishment (not concussions). A workout program that builds strength and wards off injury means, among other critical objectives, developing your "core" muscles in the abdomen, buttocks, and lower back.

Why is a strong core so important? Because the core muscles are the most powerful in the body. Moreover, the vital core is instrumental in rendering stability and balance to bodily movements as well as furnishing the wellspring from which all power emanates. For example, when a pitcher pitches, the real power does not originate in the arm and shoulder, but rather in the core. Without core work, arm and shoulder power remains mediocre.

What's more, there's evidence that strengthening core muscles might help you prevent injury. One study found, for example, that a strong core can help prevent injuries to the "lower extremities," and another discovered that among injured runners, the ones who incorporated certain core exercises into their rehabilitation program were able to get back to running more quickly than the individuals who did not. In this chapter, we'll look at some exercises that are specifically designed to help you train your core muscles, and also discuss how to prevent injury.

## Exercises to Build Your Core

In his excellent book *Warrior Cardio*, Martin Rooney includes the following cardio/CrossFit exercises that strengthen the core: arm-over-arm rope pull, sled push, rowing machine, tire flips, sledgehammer swings hitting the tire, medicine ball drills, kettlebell swings, and straight-leg lifts in a hanging position. These types of exercises work the arms, the shoulders and, particularly, the core region. In the above context, we would add light but rapid punching of the heavy bag for a series of thirty-second stints. Fluidly explosive plyometric jump-training movements such as jump squats (frog leaps) over a thirty-to-forty meter distance, repeated a given number of times, make you feel lighter on your feet when you next run. They build power and speed; they make running feel more explosive, and help prevent injury.

Though this book highlights innovative plyometric and cardio versions of core work such as frog leaps and running up steep hills (jog down with care), it does not lose sight of the fact that "classic" core movements such as the squat, the box squat, the deadlift, and the bench press, if done with proper form, are extremely core-worthy. Whether your goal involves jumping, lifting, throwing, or changing direction, the above "classic" core exercises should not be overlooked. Of course, you need to carefully calibrate the weight and repetition factors in order to avoid injury.

In addition, try the following variation of the Fartlek training method. Warm up well on a 400-meter track. Run all-out for thirty meters, stop, do three squats, jog easily for thirty meters, do three more squats, and then go back to an all-out thirty meters plus squats. Repeat the pattern all the way around the track. Rest and then, depending on your conditioning, do a number of additional laps.

Pulling a fairly heavy weight for short bursts, sprinting up steep hills, sprinting up stadium steps, performing frog leaps of thirty to forty yards, repeated four to seven times, hopping on sand with one leg, and then the other, are all fine methods of increasing explosiveness and strength. Running in place as fast as possible for fifteen to thirty seconds is, likewise, effective when done between upper-body barbell and dumbbell exercise sets.

Beyond frog leaps, sand-hopping on one leg, and the like, we suggest trying vertical leaps with arms pointing to the sky, holding a medicine ball; or leaping onto medium-sized "boxes," followed in time with taller boxes. (Medium and tall-box jumping necessitates two spotters, in case of a fall.) Other plyometric training elements are double-leg butt kicks, lateral two-leg hops, and lateral side-stepping up a sixty- or seventy-meter hill. To do this last exercise, face sideways to the hill. Extend the lead leg up the hill and close with the back leg. Continue in this manner to the top of the hill. Walk or jog back down and face in the opposite direction. Repeat until your legs feel the burn. This training technique is excellent for football backfield personnel, improving their ability to explode laterally when they're about to be tackled.

The authors of this book strive to propose a wide variety of exercise modes. If you as an athlete stubbornly repeat the same type of exercises day after day, you will adapt to them to the point that the exercises begin to lose their effectiveness. Thus, varying workout content will, over the long run, better ensure improvement in your performance results. As a bonus, you will avoid monotony and discouragement.

Up to this point, we have stressed thinking out of the box to create original types of workout elements, some of which can be categorized as CrossFit or plyometric/core exercises. There exist novel training approaches that target body movements related to the skill-set of a particular sport. These generally come under the heading of "functional fitness." Consider the off-season functional fitness regimen of Drew Brees, the New Orleans Saints' quarterback. Instead of squats, bench presses, and working with conventional gym equipment, Brees spent several hours a day during the summer of 2015 working on his functional fitness; that is, "replicating the movements and isolating the muscle groups he most relies on as a quarterback. Rather than trying to bulk up, his focus was on flexibility, core stability and rotational strength," as *Sports Illustrated* explained it. Brees concentrated on core work with elastic bands, given that throwing a football with speed and accuracy involves the core more than it does the arm. Next came a series of CrossFit-like exercises with battling ropes. Among other "functional" movements, Brees participated in a type of handball game that developed reaction time and hand/eye coordination. Each station of his daily workout produced fatigue but ensured that Brees would be ready for the season—which, because it requires him to watch film and attend strategy sessions, might not allow for repeated, extensive gym work.

This novel approach is an improvement over past training methods. Back in the old days, in order to get stronger, the ambitious athlete did heavy weights and long reps, resting in between sets. This was very hard on the athlete's joints and even caused a lot of careers to end by blowing out knees and backs. Over time this type of lifting can also lead to the onset of arthritis.

A word now on an exercise routine that covers non-core muscle groups. We have found that the best way to get stronger with less stress on your joints is to pick a body part you are working on, on a particular day, and set up four exercise stations for that body part. Covering the four exercise stations equals one rotation. Three rotations is the goal. Find a weight that challenges you but does not put a strain on the joints or back, and do twenty reps with proper form. If your form starts to get sloppy, reduce the weight you are lifting, because the exercise must always be done with proper form.

Then pick a type of cardio that you will perform immediately after the four exercise stations have been covered. This should be something like jumping rope, touching toes on step, riding a stationary bicycle, jumping jacks, or doing "mountain climbers." Keep this method and start a rotation by going to one station after the other, performing twenty reps per station. Once you're past the fourth station, go right into two minutes of cardio. Athletes need to learn to pace themselves through the two-minute cardio routine. This will teach you to control breathing when in tense situations. The most strenuous exercises should be incorporated only after you have achieved a high level of conditioning.

In the second rotation, the twenty reps should be getting more difficult to complete. If you can still do twenty reps then you probably didn't choose a heavy enough weight on the first rotation. Again, on the third rotation you should barely be able to get ten reps. When you can work up to twenty reps at each station for three rotations, increase the weight by five or ten pounds and, after a two- or three-day break, start the process all over again, with twenty reps on the first rotation, fifteen on the second, and ten on the third. Keep a careful record of the weight you are using. The gradual increase in weight represents the key to great physical progress. Remember to include rest days.

The above training regimens aim to help you strengthen your core as well as other muscle groups. By doing so, you improve your balance, stability, and explosiveness, making it easier to perform at the top of your game in any sport. Moreover, having a strong core should make you less susceptible to injury.

## Preventing Injury

One of the most profound questions related to sport injuries is how to prevent them, particularly at the college and professional levels. This holds true for contact as well as non-contact sports. The issue raised here is vast, and this chapter does not pretend to be comprehensive. However, it is hoped that the following will be helpful in preventing joint (ligament, tendon) and articulation-type injuries.

The best way to introduce this vast subject is to refer to the seventeenth-century French author, La Fontaine, and his fable "The Oak and the Reed." Succinctly put, the fable goes something like the following: "When the hurricane winds came, the stately, proud Oak was severely damaged, while the lowly Reed survived intact." The key line of the fable, spoken by the Reed, reads as follows: "I bend but do not break." The moral of the fable as applied to our subject is that injury can be better prevented when strength and size are combined with flexibility.

To prevent injury, you need to be like the Reed: flexible enough to bend but not brittle enough to break. In the context of the present chapter, the "reed" can be visualized in human terms as an arm, a leg, or the body as a whole. The "reed" not only bends under extreme weather conditions, but has a spring-like action that combines strength, flexibility, and speed. To achieve these qualities, the elite athlete needs to view free-weight and stationary machine training as only one part of a much more comprehensive approach to workouts. This training strategy is centered on plyometric and CrossFit exercises: rope manipulation, core and full-body drilling movements such as frog-leaping, sand hopping, one-legged squats, rope climbing, hill and stadium-step running, medicine-ball training, and change-of-direction movements. This type of conditioning is at the heart of an injury-prevention strategy as well as representing the groundwork for powerful yet fluid explosiveness. For a visual insight into what we are driving at here, go online to view the workouts of freestyle wrestler and world champion, Jordan Burroughs.

In the context of injury prevention, let us think about, for example, the preventive measures that help preclude trauma to the ACL (anterior cruciate ligament). First of all, universally-accepted exercises that work the legs, glutes, hips, and specific muscles that support and stabilize the knee are essential in preventing a torn ACL. Secondly, plyometric movements such as frog-leap sets of thirty yards or more, box jumping (with two spotters), step-ups, single-leg hops, burpees, lunges, skater plyos (side-to-side sliding movements), and the like, are excellent for all-around conditioning as well as knee strengthening. Experts report that jumping rope is another excellent preventive measure. The above knee-related strategies can be applied, with modifications, to help prevent injury to other vulnerable parts of the body such as the shoulder and ankle. Interestingly, we have found that leg injuries that prevent running may not impede you from riding a stationary bike, jogging in a pool, or even walking for fairly long distances. However, the feasibility of practicing such exercises depends on the severity of the injury. A groin pull, for example, restricts most sustained movement and needs a relatively protracted time period to heal.

Tendonitis is a repetitive stress/overuse injury and should be treated with ice and rest. If ice and rest do not seem to help, then try a hot tub with pulsating jets. We have noticed that the hot tub with pulsating jets is an excellent therapy for plantar fasciitis. Of course, when the injury does not respond to self-remedy it is time to see a health-care professional who can provide you with a set of rehabilitative exercises and other treatments.

As mentioned in other chapters, the athlete aspiring to elite status or full potential should focus on tried-and-true, as well as safe, innovation-driven strategies that will allow the individual in question to excel. One example, not included above, suffices here. For balance, stamina, and hip strength, stand on one foot, lift the free knee to the perpendicular or just above, lower it back to the ground, and then extend the same leg laterally and back down. Try one set of thirty to fifty movements; switch legs, and then repeat. In time, you should be able to complete two rotations (having worked both legs twice at fifty repetitions).

When speaking with a professional rehabilitation therapist, he mentioned to us that a stretching warm-up was actually counterproductive with regards to possible injury. Warming down, however, was essential. From personal experience, we would have to disagree on the first point. To move right into exercise without first warming up and then stretching is not a good idea. It is hard to imagine, for example, a martial artist doing leg kicks against a heavy bag or a football player kicking field goals without first warming up and then stretching thoroughly.

Most injuries are a by-product of the conflict between goal-oriented ambition and reasonableness. All-out workouts, all the time, inexorably lead to heartbreaking injury. A practical example: One morning during the off-season, a runner named Winston works out the legs (calf, quads, hamstrings) on stationary machines and then tops the workout on a stairclimber which he prefers to the elliptical machine. Winston stair-steps for twenty minutes. He is exhausted and, without cooling down, heads for the showers. After a wholesome lunch and a nap, Winston converses with a series of friends on his cell phone. At 3:20 p.m. he is back at the fitness center where he has a session scheduled with his professional trainer, Denise.

Unexpectedly, Denise arrives early, preventing Winston from warming up and stretching adequately. Due to inclement weather, she has Winston begin his workout indoors with a variety of cardiovascular routines, beginning with squats, lunges, and step-ups. Winston, following her instructions, then performs a series of butt-kicks. In the middle of one of these, Winston experiences a searing pain on the inside of his left thigh. His first reaction is to continue the butt-kicks. Impossible! Denise calls over a physiotherapist friend who consoles Winston by assessing the damage as minimal. He is told to go home and ice the injury, which should get better in three days.

The therapist is far from accurate in his diagnosis. Winston, in fact, is suffering from the early, deceptive symptoms of a serious groin pull. The following morning Winston is unable to walk. What is the two-part moral of this story? First, you need to be vigilant about not continually overtraining the same parts of the body, particularly if your core muscles are not in good shape. Second, always warm up and stretch before working out.

The best way to prevent injuries related to running, skiing, power-lifting, etc. is to develop core strength and general body flexibility. Winston, as we remember, had little time to warm up. Moreover, he did not work his core muscles on a regular basis. Lastly, Winston had worked the thigh area just that morning.

Also, a heart rate monitor (HRM) can be an effective tool for runners to prevent overtraining injuries. For those athletes who are comfortable with computer technology, it is first necessary to find your maximum heart rate (MHR). With this knowledge in hand, you can monitor your runs as follows: 65% of MHR or less equates with an easy Sunday run; a 65% to 85% effort represents aerobic endurance pace; 85% to 95% of MHR is the lactate threshold zone in which aerobic training effort is at its maximum and, therefore, the most beneficial. Anything above 95% of MHR is consistent with developing the anaerobic system (all-out running, for example).

We cannot overemphasize the importance of consistently exercising and strengthening the core. Perhaps the best way to illustrate this latter point is to imagine an elite athlete in any sport who pulls an abdominal muscle. The result? An inability to participate in competitions or to work out normally. A pulled abdominal muscle produces a state of near-paralysis that makes even normal breathing or sneezing difficult.

We should point out that proper core training does not necessarily always prevent injury. When this happens despite your careful precautions, it's important to maintain a positive attitude about rehabilitation. Let us close this chapter with a word from Jordan Burroughs, an Olympic and world wrestling champion who has gone through his share of injuries. "I want to challenge anyone who's had an injury to remain hungry," he writes. "I know your pain. I've been there. Stay focused. Surround yourself with positive people. When the injury heals, work as hard as is safely possible and picture where you want to be, not where you are. Who cares how good you were before the injury? Work to be better. Adversity doesn't build character, it reveals it."

## KEY TAKEAWAYS

- Training your core muscles (abdomen, buttocks, and lower back) will provide you with greater strength, balance, and flexibility.

- Core exercises are the key to avoiding injury, as long as you first warm up adequately and follow the safe warmup with a thorough stretching session.

# 10

# Nutrition Matters: Top Four Super Foods for Peak Performance

*Let food be thy medicine and medicine be thy food.*

—Hippocrates

**TO BECOME LEAN**, gain the right type of muscle, and consistently feel great before workouts, you should know which and how much protein, carbohydrate, and unsaturated fat to consume daily; how often you should eat; and the amount of liquid you need to properly hydrate. By doing so, you are more likely to reach your full athletic potential. To this end, have on-hand a long list of varied healthy, nutrient-filled foods and snacks to eat. Know, moreover, which foods are the most desirable and which ones to avoid at all costs.

In this chapter we will explore some general nutritional advice for athletes and also take a moment to highlight and define the nature of "super foods," so called because they are nutrient-rich and considered to be especially beneficial for health and well-being. Athletes need to treat their bodies like a high-performance Formula One car. If we put junk in it, the car will spit and sputter and eventually even break down. With proper "nutrition" the car will perform at its best. When we step on the gas, we will feel power and speed and be able to shift smoothly into overdrive. Likewise, healthy food will help our bodies and minds to perform in a dominant manner when we are training or competing.

## You Are What You Eat

Pushing our bodies to attain excellence entails more than high-quality training and mind control; it also requires smart, appropriate eating and drinking. If we treat our bodies like everyone else does, then we will also perform like them. We want to be better than everyone else! Our goal is to set ourselves apart. That is why we do not have excess fat to weigh us down. We are lean and built for strength, speed, endurance, agility, and explosiveness.

So we focus on eating the Good Stuff, which is a healthy balance of the three building blocks of the diet: carbohydrates (including fruits, vegetables, and whole grains); fats; and proteins. Fruits and vegetables are important in any diet for athletes as they contain a host of vitamins and minerals. Aim to get between 45 to 60 percent of your daily calorie intake from carbs, but know that not all carbs are created equal. White breads, for example, do almost nothing to help your body, nor does soda or sugary food. If, by chance, you are a fan of processed and fast food, imbibe sugary drinks, eat candy, and so on, you will perform at less than maximum ability. You want your carbs to come from fruits (not sugary fruit juices), vegetables, and "whole" grains, such as high-fiber breads and cereals. Despite the recent trend of diets that tell you to avoid all carbohydrates, they should still be your diet's basic foundation. Don't stop eating *all* carbs just because *some* kinds of carbs are bad for you. A study from a 2004 edition of the *Journal of Sports Sciences* found no evidence to show that a high-fat diet that restricted carbohydrate intake had any benefit over a typical higher-carb regimen. Good vegetables to consume include zucchini, cauliflower, asparagus, broccoli, celery, leeks, and cucumber; good fruits are apples, kiwis, mangoes, pineapples, papayas, strawberries, and blueberries.

While vegetables and fruits contain nutrients that your body needs, you also need some amount of fat in your diet. Vitamins A, D, E, and K are fat-soluble vitamins, meaning they are better absorbed and utilized in the presence of fat. Not only that, fat plays a role in cell membrane structure and hormone production, keeping you healthy and performing at your best. The amount of fat required each day depends on your overall calorie intake. The Iowa State University Extension and Outreach recommends that twenty to thirty-five percent of your total daily calorie consumption should come from fat. For an athlete consuming 2,600 calories per day, this would mean getting between 60 and 100 grams of fat. Stick mainly to unsaturated fats found in fish, nuts, and natural products like olive oil, avocado, and olives.

The final category in your diet is protein. The safest approach is to eat lean meats, such as skinless chicken or fish, each with abundant helpings of dark vegetables. Another excellent source of protein is derived from the whites of eggs. If you are eating out at a restaurant such as Subway, ask for tuna fish with abundant helpings of olives, onion, lettuce, and spinach.

Remember, we are the product of what we put into our bodies. Try the following for several days: drink water instead of sodas; eat fish and lean meats such as skinless chicken; and consume dark vegetables and salads with a light helping of olive oil, grains, nuts, and fruits. Notice how you sleep better, lose weight (if desired), feel energized, and are thinking clearly and positively. Now, the engine is operating at maximum speed and efficiency. Swimming or running becomes so much more smoothly explosive. You feel great and can't wait to show your stuff, whether you are training or competing.

We are emphasizing good nutrition for both physical and psychological reasons. Obviously, healthy food provides the aspiring athlete with energy as well as healing properties. What is often overlooked, however, is the psychological effect good food choices can have. When you're in training and you consistently eat healthy food, avoiding rich desserts, sodas, fast food, fatty meats, and so on, you wake up feeling refreshed and ready to go. You're more likely to undertake all the prescribed sets of exercises, each with proper form and the planned number of repetitions. Imagine arriving at your workout locale feeling fresh and positive instead of somewhat sluggish. Of course, no matter how well you eat and sleep, there will be mornings when you wake up stiff and tired. This is to be expected. Eating correctly will reduce drastically the days when you are feeling below par.

A word about certain aspects of a "Mediterranean Diet" as it relates to athletes is appropriate here. This manner of eating is heart-healthy, has a positive effect on joints, and reduces inflammation. The plan forgoes sweets and is stingy when it comes to saturated fat and processed food. Moreover, it welcomes olive oil. Legumes such as kidney, black, and many other beans plus nuts and seeds are encouraged. Fish, such as salmon and tuna, are prominent in this system since they benefit the heart and the lungs. Whole grains such as oats, rye, quinoa, brown rice, and whole wheat, along with fruits and vegetables of a rich, dark color, make up the core of the Mediterranean Diet. These nutrients are full of antioxidants.

## Timing Your Meals for Peak Performance

Your pre-workout/pre-performance meal can help supply the body with the significant amount of energy you need. However, it will not provide all of it, so it won't work to just eat one healthy meal right before a competition. Instead, you should consume the right types of food for several days prior to any event in order to charge the muscles with plenty of glycogen, the energy source your muscles use during most sporting activities. Ideally you should be eating well at all times. The pre-game meal will help to stabilize blood sugar levels, hydrate the body, and prevent gastrointestinal upset. No one meal or food is right for every athlete, but some choices are smarter than others.

Timing the meal is one of the keys to your success. Most studies show that if you eat the meal at least three hours prior to the event or training session, you then achieve better results. It is also important to eat the right combination of foods to ensure that the stomach is empty and there is no excess gas or gastrointestinal upset at game or event time. The latest research indicates that eating some protein and carbohydrate one-half hour before physical activity and within a half-hour after exertion is a smart strategy.

Post-competition meals of an average athlete often consist of pizza with a beer or soda, but elite athletes think differently. They start preparing for the next event as soon as the previous competition is over, making their postgame meal as nutritious as the pre-game one. Champions always focus on the goal and task ahead. Self-discipline rules.

Some guides to high-level performance nutrition speak of allowing yourself one "cheat" meal per week. In principle this may not be a bad idea. However, in reality, "pigging out" may instantly add unwanted pounds to your weight and may also condition your taste buds and appetite to continue to eat in a less than ideal manner in the days following a binge meal. Soda intake is particularly dangerous, since its consumption is addictive.

## The Four Super Foods

The following super foods can help fuel your body to reach the peak performance you have envisioned and planned for yourself. The authors of this book have decided to feature only four "super foods" for the super-athlete. These four foods were chosen because they are often overlooked in sport nutrition-oriented volumes, as well as books dealing with healthy food.

Let us begin with a whole-grain, unrefined cereal: **brown rice.** We could have also chosen buckwheat, barley, or millet. Particularly if it is chewed well, it is easily digested. It is a high-quality carbohydrate full of vitamins and minerals. Brown rice (along with proper medicine) is recommended for the relief of diarrhea. As opposed to white rice it does not lose its B vitamins, phosphorus, iron, manganese, and other nutrients during the milling process. Moreover, brown rice appears to have a beneficial effect on your health by lowering blood pressure and protecting against kidney stones. It is rich in antioxidants such as selenium. From personal experience, we would not recommend eating brown rice in the days preceding an important competition. Initially, if you have not been eating it on a regular basis, it has a temporary constipating effect. However, if chewed well and eaten every day or so, it has a beneficial effect on digestion.

As with brown rice, **garbanzo beans** (also known as chick peas), are extremely high in caloric value and possess abundant vitamins (A, B, C) and minerals (calcium, iron, phosphorus). They are digested easily and are a significant source of protein. They are a popular dish in the Middle East where they are often combined with garlic, lemon juice, and tahini, or ground into hummus and eaten with pita bread. The Ancient Greeks and Romans enjoyed their taste and texture. Worldwide, garbanzo beans are the most popular legume. They are a fixture of American salad bars. The superior athlete can profit from their rich supply of dietary fiber which, in turn, aids the digestive system and enhances heart health. One word of caution: garbanzo beans are not the easiest food to prepare. For example, they need to be soaked overnight and the outer membrane must be removed after cooking and before eating. Follow directions carefully, or allow a friend or family member to help you get used to preparing the beans the right way.

The third super food is **nuts**: walnuts, almonds, pecans, filberts and the like. Nuts serve as a perfect snack food, particularly right after a hard workout. Rather than eating a factory-processed nutrition bar, nuts are a wiser substitute. Admittedly, you should take care to chew nuts slowly and thoroughly. Let us look specifically at almonds, which contain vitamins B1, B2, and niacin. Their mineral content includes calcium, iron, phosphorus, potassium, and magnesium. Moreover, they provide a significant blend of carbohydrate, fat, and protein. In *The Encyclopedia of Fruits, Vegetables, Nuts and Seeds for Healthy Living*, Joseph M. Kadans writes: "Almonds and almond butter are very nourishing foods and are recognized as muscle builders. The high fat, carbohydrate and protein content make it an ideal food for strengthening the body when there is no need to worry about the increase in the supply of fat. The content of calcium makes it valuable for the teeth and bones. Almonds are delicious as substitutes for candy or other sweets, but these nuts are also popular for cooking in [ … ] breads, as well as in fruit and vegetable salads."

The fourth and last super food to be featured here is a carbohydrate: **shallots**. Surprisingly, a perusal of major nutrition-oriented publications results in the near-total absence of the word "shallots." Why this is the case appears to be a mystery.

Shallots belong to the Allium family of foods, which also includes onions, garlic, and chives. Shallots possess more flavonoid antioxidants, vitamins, and minerals than onions. They reduce cholesterol levels and hardening of the arteries while functioning as an anti-inflammatory, anti-allergic, anti-fungal, and anti-viral agent. Moreover, shallots contain organosulfur compounds that help protect against stomach and colorectal cancers, while helping to lower blood sugar levels in diabetics.

Shallots possess a richer concentration of vitamins and minerals than onions. Vitamins include A (a super anti-oxidant known for its salubrious effect in helping impede lung and oral cavity cancers), and folic acid (known for its positive influence on brain function and mood stability). Other vitamins include B6, C, thiamin, and pantothenic acid. With regards to minerals, shallots are high in potassium (a contributor to healthy heart, kidney, and muscle function), iron, calcium, copper, selenium, manganese, and phosphorous.

If you enjoy cooking, keep the powerful nutritional values of shallots in mind. Lightly cooked or raw shallots can be introduced into salads, gravy, stews, and soups as a substitute for onions. They are low in calories, cholesterol, sodium, and saturated fat while being high in fiber and protein. In today's world, they are particularly attractive to those athletes seeking to lose weight. To avoid eye irritation, it is wise to soak the trimmed bulbs in cold water before chopping, or use a mechanical chopper.

## Rethinking Breakfast

Let us speak about breakfast, the most critical meal of the day. Years ago, a big breakfast with bacon, sausage, and eggs was very popular in the United States. It is still the staple of hotel breakfast buffets. Unfortunately, the regular consumption of such a breakfast leads to premature heart disease and artery blockage. Instead we suggest the following healthy types of breakfast food combinations.

- Fresh fruit in season (blueberries are a good option) with raw nuts, Swiss *muesli* (granola), and a dab of yogurt with 2 percent fat.

- Oatmeal or raw oats mixed in with any of the fruits detailed here.

- Banana slices, chopped dates, berries, raw walnuts or raw almonds, and a dab of 2 percent yogurt.

- Fresh fruit in season mixed with no-sugar *muesli* and a mix of raw nuts and honey.

- As regards breakfast drinks, freshly-squeezed orange juice is an excellent choice. A fair intake of coffee is also a possibility, or a mix of coffee and chicory (available pre-mixed). Attempt not to add sugar to your coffee or (herbal) tea.

If you are addicted to eggs, bacon, and sausage, skip the bacon and sausage and prepare four or five eggs sunny-side-up. Eliminate the egg yolks and create an egg sandwich with multi-grain bread. With regard to egg yolks, the American Heart Journal suggests you can "safely eat two eggs a day without negatively affecting [ ... ] blood pressure, cholesterol, or body weight." Other scientific findings demonstrate the opposite. To be safe, eat two to four eggs a week if they are to your liking. A word of caution: placing raw eggs in a shake drink invites the risk of salmonella poisoning.

## Water, Sports Drinks, and Signs of Dehydration

Let us turn to the question of hydration. Whether you're a serious athlete or a recreational exerciser, it's important to make sure you get the right amount of water before, during, and after exercising. Water regulates your body temperature, lubricates joints and helps transport nutrients for energy and general health. If you're not properly hydrated, then your body will be unable to perform at its highest level, and you may experience fatigue, muscle cramps, dizziness or the more serious symptoms of dehydration.

There are no set guidelines for water intake while exercising because every individual is different. Sweat, heat, humidity, exercise intensity, and duration are just some of the variables that must be considered. A simple way to make sure you're staying properly hydrated is to check your urine. If it is consistently colorless or light yellow, you are most likely staying well hydrated. Dark yellow or amber-colored urine is a sign of dehydration. Remember, however, that too much liquid consumption is harmful.

The American Council on Fitness has suggested the following basic water intake guidelines for people doing moderate to high-intensity exercise:

- Drink seventeen to twenty ounces of water two to three hours before you start exercising.

- Drink eight ounces of water twenty to thirty minutes before you start exercising or during your warm-up.

- Drink seven to ten ounces of water every twenty minutes during rigorous training.

- Drink a minimum of eight ounces of water no more than thirty minutes after you exercise. If the atmosphere is warm or hot, adjust upward accordingly.

To obtain a more specific measurement of how much water you should be drinking, you can measure your sweat loss. To this end, weigh yourself on a digital scale before and after you exercise. Any weight loss you experience is most likely from fluid loss and needs to be replaced with water. Record this number and use it as a guide for how much you need to be drinking while you exercise. Drink sixteen to twenty-four ounces of water for every pound of body weight you lose while exercising. (Helpful hint: a gallon weighs about eight pounds, a quart weighs about two pounds, and a pint weighs about one pound.) This approach to estimating water needs is especially useful for high endurance athletes, such as individuals who run marathons.

When exercising, water is the best drink for most people, most of the time. However, if you are exercising at a high intensity for more than an hour, you may want to choose a sports drink. The calories, potassium, and other nutrients in sport drinks can help provide energy and electrolytes to ensure you perform adequately for a longer period of time. Choose sports drinks wisely, as they are often high in calories, sugar, and sodium. Also check the serving size—one bottle may contain several servings. Some sports drinks contain caffeine. If you use a sports drink that contains caffeine, be careful not to get too high a dose of it in your diet. Some sports nutritionists recommend diluting sports drinks with water. If you regularly hydrate with a sports drink, remember that it likely contains refined sugars, artificial colors, chemicals, and artificial flavors. A substitute for sports drinks is coconut water, which contains no fat and little sodium, is rich in potassium, and supplies healthy doses of vitamin C, calcium, phosphorus, and magnesium. It does not provide protein.

You should be able to recognize the signs of dehydration, which occurs when you lose more fluid than you drink. When your body does not have enough water, it does not function properly. Dehydration can range from mild to severe. The signs of dehydration can include:

- Dizziness or lightheadedness

- Nausea or vomiting

- Muscle cramps

- Dry mouth

- Sweating stops

- Heart pain and palpitations

Hydration should not be taken lightly. On hot days, in particular, it is crucial. Signs of severe dehydration can include mental confusion, dizziness, and fainting. If you have any of these symptoms, go to the emergency room immediately. Severe symptoms can lead to an inability of the body to cool itself. The three stages of heat illness are heat cramps, heat exhaustion, and heatstroke. Heat cramps can affect the abdomen and limbs. Heat exhaustion is more serious and can include feeling faint or experiencing nausea, headache, rapid pulse, and low blood pressure. The most serious heat-related illness is heatstroke. Symptoms can include high body temperature, rapid pulse, flushed skin, lack of sweating, rapid breathing, and possibly even delirium, loss of consciousness, or seizures. Seek immediate emergency medical attention if you experience heatstroke. Untreated, it can lead to death. If you participate in marathons and triathlons, drinking adequately before, during, and after the competition is an absolute must, especially on hot days. I (Dan Valahu) learned the above lessons the hard way. On a particularly hot July day in Waco, Texas, I participated in a marathon. After finishing, I became faint and needed emergency help to recover. Initially, nothing, including an ice bath seemed to work. Finally, two cold cokes did the trick.

As mentioned above, there is danger in drinking too much liquid just as there is danger in drinking too little. There have been instances where athletes have actually drunk too much and died from overhydration, or "water intoxication." According to the *New York Times,* the latest science indicates that dehydration during low intensity sport activity is rarely if ever dangerous, but overhydration unquestionably is. The overall evidence, however, still dictates that you need to be adequately hydrated before, during, and following long-distance endurance events, particularly on hot, humid days.

## Foods to Avoid

So far in this chapter we have stayed positive by pointing to all the good things you should be eating and drinking for optimal health and outstanding sports performance. It's time to spend a little time on the flip side: the eating-related habits you should avoid.

- Keep away from roasted, highly-salted nuts that today are popular as snacks. Nuts are healthy in and of themselves, but not if you add large amounts of salt and sugar.

- Don't eat the evening meal at a late hour; try to make your last meal of the day a relatively light one.

- Avoid drinking during lunch and dinner. Instead, drink water or other healthy liquids fifteen to thirty minutes before the meal. Liquid intake with meals dilutes the digestive juices.

- At a social event where food is displayed, try to shun the greasy options while choosing raw food such as carrots and celery sticks. If you are sure the fruit has been well washed, choose it for dessert rather than eating the cookies and pastry.

- Avoid hydrogenated fats like margarine and lard. Olive oil is better.

- Steer clear of meals that are unbalanced; that is, which lack the appropriate mix of carbohydrate, protein, and fat.

- Pass by the red meat and processed meats such as sausage, salami, and meat pies in favor of skinless chicken, game, fowl, and lean meats such as turkey. For example, it appears that meat from grass-fed bison or buffalo contains omega-3, which is good for you, and contains less fat than normal beef.

- Don't consume too much salt. Potato chips are one of the main culprits here.

- Circumvent pesticide residue by buying organic produce if it's available and you can afford it. If you're buying prepackaged produce, check the mandatory content label to see whether it contains chemicals, flavorings, additives, and so on.

- Stay away from brightly-colored cakes, ice cream, candies, and soft drinks. They are chock full of dye, fat, and sugar. Initially, it may seem difficult to pass on dessert. However, if you can hold off for a few days or a week, your desire for sweets will have vanished.

- Forget about "energy" drinks. They are problematic.

- Again, avoid dessert and sodas altogether. By doing so, weight management becomes much easier. Weigh yourself daily. Keeping track provides insight into what foods to avoid and the results of overeating.

This chapter has dealt with healthy eating as it relates to serious athletes in their quest for elite status. Smart food choices made now, daily, will not only positively affect mood and motivation, but will help ensure a healthy life once your competing days are over. Establishing good habits now will lower your chances later of hypertension (high blood pressure), cardiovascular disease, diabetes, obesity, acid reflux, osteoporosis, and a whole host of other modern-day afflictions that, partly or mainly because of poor eating habits, are prevalent in our society. The sooner the outstanding athlete becomes aware of the healthy way of eating, the better.

## KEY TAKEAWAYS

- Always remind yourself: You are what you eat.

- Adopting a healthy eating philosophy that focuses on vegetables, whole grains, and lean proteins while excluding sodas and desserts is easier than you think.

- Pay attention to the timing of your meals as well as to their content.

- Drink sufficient liquid but avoid drinking too much. Be particularly attentive to proper hydration in hot, humid weather.

# PART 3

# THE PSYCHOLOGY OF THE ELITE ATHLETE

# 11

# Never Give in to Adversity

*The most important thing a player must have is mental toughness. [ … ] When you want something really badly, don't give up until you've got it.*

—Mia Hamm

**AMERICAN MIXED MARTIAL ARTIST HOLLY HOLM** experienced the depths of defeat on a December night in 2011. In the ring against French fighter Anne Sophie Mathis, the bantamweight Holm endured the worst beating of her extensive professional boxing career. Holm could have given up and simply retired. Instead, she accepted a rematch with Mathis.

On a summer evening in 2012, fighting in the same New Mexico Route 66 Casino where Mathis first roughed her up, the Albuquerque resident turned the tables on the French boxer, winning by decision in the seventh round. Having convincingly exorcised her demons, Holm was ready for a battle with twenty-eight-year old Ronda Rousey, an undefeated mixed martial artist, the world's champion in the bantamweight class. Jabs to the face kept Rousey away until a kick to the side of the head knocked Rousey out. We can say that the celebratory parade in Albuquerque in Holm's honor was more than appropriate; it was totally justified. Holm was an 18-to-1 underdog going into the octagon with Rousey, and she left it with a new championship belt. It was one of the greatest upsets in the history of the sport.

Holm exemplified some of the necessary psychological traits of successful elite athletes: She did not give in to adversity or defeat; she adapted her goal to her changing circumstances, and she refused to be intimidated by an allegedly "unbeatable" opponent. In this chapter, we'll explore these traits in depth.

## Never Give Up

Olympic wrestler Doug Blubaugh was in great shape heading into the 1960 Summer Olympic Games in Rome. He had worked so hard that his weight on match day was down to 152 pounds in the 157-pound weight class. Gary Simons, Blubaugh's teammate on the 1960 freestyle-wrestling Olympic team, trained with him in Colorado during the lead-up to the Games. "We were running all the time—long, hard runs with weights on our legs in the high altitude," Simons recalled. "Some of the guys were about dying. [ … ] I went up to him [Blubaugh] and asked if they were trying to kill us?" Blubaugh answered, "Simons, they can't make it tough enough for me. I love this! Give me more." Blubaugh's strategy was to survive the most arduous training imaginable to ensure that he could successfully meet any challenge in the Olympic matches themselves, including a near-certain one against the five-time world champion: Iranian wrestler Emamali Habibi.

As the Olympic semifinal match against Habibi began, the latter dominated with two explosive moves, winning back points and forcing Blubaugh to escape, having to employ a neck bridge in each instance. But the ever-optimistic, unbending Blubaugh was in no mood to give up. A minute later, as Habibi moved in for a third and possibly match-ending move on Blubaugh, the American had had enough. Supremely confident, despite being in a precarious position points-wise, Blubaugh caught Habibi and pancaked him. For a minute and a half Habibi struggled mightily to escape, but Blubaugh had him in an ever-tightening vise that led to a pin. Blubaugh went on to win the finals and earn Olympic glory.

So, no matter the challenge, focus all your mental and physical energies toward victory, despite the odds. Prepare well, and then go all out. Do not give up, either in training or in competition. Even if you are up against the "best" in the world, do your focused, determined best, without fear. Think of Doug Blubaugh.

Think also of Jean Claude Killy, the modern era's greatest skier, whose never-give-up determination brought him all three alpine gold medals in the 1968 Winter Olympic Games. Just before the downhill in 1968, Killy's skis lost all their special wax in warmup. Properly waxed skis allows for less friction between skis and snow or ice. What was Killy's attitude to the loss of the all-important wax? He flew out of the gate and took every risk imaginable. He won the downhill by the slimmest of margins and then went on to victory in the slalom and giant slalom. His philosophy relative to competitive skiing was simply never to give up, which is excellent advice nearly fifty years later. Like Killy, never complain; assert yourself with determination despite what others might think. Show courage, energy, and self-confidence. Be bold. Be completely focused on doing your absolute best. Jean-Claude Killy had to maintain a confident, winning attitude over a one-week, three-event schedule. He did not permit pressure to build up as he waited for the giant slalom and slalom events. He stood firm in his belief in himself, despite the above-cited problem with his skis and regardless of the foggy and icy weather conditions.

Never give in, particularly if the adversary appears to be unbeatable. This unbeatable individual is supremely confident, sometimes unwisely so. To illustrate this point let us look at the heavyweight boxing reign of Floyd Patterson. From 1956 to 1959 Patterson easily disposed of a series of adversaries to retain his heavyweight title. But in 1959, Sweden's undefeated heavyweight, Ingemar Johansson, loomed on the horizon.

Johansson was a somewhat awkward fighter but he had a devastating straight right hand that most of his opponents never saw coming. In time, Johansson's bread and butter punch became known as "lightning and thunder." Once the contract to fight Patterson was signed, Johansson, who had little regard for the champion and his peek-a-boo style of defense, furnished *Sports Illustrated* with a multi-page graphic preview of how he was going to knock Patterson out with his "lightning and thunder" straight right hand.

On the night of June 26, 1959, Johansson and Patterson stepped into a makeshift ring on the old Yankee Stadium grounds. Patterson appeared bored; Johansson was ready. In the third round the Swede knocked Patterson down as he had predicted, with a powerful, straight right. The champion went down, rising only to be put down a second time. By the two-minute mark, Patterson had hit the canvas an incredible seven times. The referee had by then seen enough. With his hands waving, the referee stepped in between the fighters and stopped the fight, awarding a technical knockout to Johansson, the new heavyweight champion of the world.

Johansson is to be admired here for his confidence and his refusal to be psyched out by Patterson's prowess. But Johansson is not the only hero in this story. After months of self-imposed solitary confinement, during which Patterson suffered from a dark, depressive funk, his shame finally metamorphosed into a focused confidence. Patterson once again began to train hard, both conventionally and unconventionally, gaining eight pounds of muscle and vowing to come back. In the rematch, Patterson battered Johansson from the opening bell. In the fifth round an explosive, on-target left hook knocked Johansson out cold. Floyd Patterson overcame the odds and became the first fighter in history to regain the world heavyweight title.

## Adaptation to Surrounding Circumstances

We've made it clear that you should never give in to adversity or defeat. However, that's not to say that you shouldn't learn from these things. Think of them as tools to tell you where your natural gifts are and what you can focus on. There are athletes who should radically alter their immediate and long-term goal but, because of their stubborn nature, or a blindly inflexible coach or parent, continue to search for success in a sport not adapted to their athletic skill set. It has been painful to watch these untalented individuals fade into oblivion for lack of native ability.

On the other hand, there are elite athletes who, due to their adaptive turn of mind, recognize early that their particular quest for athletic glory is misguided. Earlier in this book, I (Dan Valahu) had the pleasure of writing about Sandy Van Kennen, the swimmer from Wesleyan University (Conn.), who was the 1966 NCAA 50-yard short-course swimming champion. As curious as it may sound, the story of one of Van Kennen's freshman-year dormitory floormates, Joseph Pickard, illustrates how a college athlete, confronted with a serious dose of adversity, decided to pivot adroitly in the direction of a new sport. In high school, the diminutive (5 ft., 4 in.) 150-lb. Pickard was captain and fullback of the football team in his senior year. As a freshman at Wesleyan, he was as fearless as ever, but was not chosen as the starting fullback. In the spring of his sophomore year, Pickard decided to abandon football and join the lacrosse team. Because of his small size and extremely quick reflexes, he gravitated toward the goalie position. In his senior year at Wesleyan, Pickard was designated all-American and was chosen as goalie of the East team in the 1966 East-West post-season national all-star game.

Due to his lack of success on the football field, Pickard could have become dejected to the point of giving up his sport-related ambitions. Instead, he adapted to the situation, thought things out, and decided to pursue lacrosse, even though he had no prior experience in the sport. Because of his natural athletic ability and because he consistently spent extra hours in the net fending off shots, he quickly developed into the best college lacrosse goalie in the land.

The moral of this story is that "never giving up" cannot always be implemented literally. Let us say, for example, that you possess superior athletic ability but, due to the particular circumstances surrounding your football team, the coach has placed you low on the backfield depth chart. What do you do? How do you react? Since you are fast, agile, and a glue-fingered pass catcher, you convince the coach to move you to the position of wide receiver. And voilà, in short order, thanks to your natural pass-catching prowess and your superior work ethic, you become not only the best receiver on the team, but "the go-to guy" in tight game situations.

Let us now turn to an unusual but true story involving two high school students, both of whom are potential track stars. Jennifer has just finished her sophomore year at a privately-funded high school to which families with or without means can send their children. Mark is a young man who is about to enter his junior year at a private college preparatory school. Both attend high schools that were founded not too long ago and therefore do not possess a track on their grounds. Both individuals are excellent students who have the full support of their parents with regard to pursuing track seriously.

But that is where the similarities end. With the help of coaches and the administration of his school, Mark is able to train at a nearby college track and compete, with special permission, in private school meets, including dual meets, on a regular basis. He has not allowed adversity to stop him from becoming one of the best 800-meter runners in Central Texas. Jennifer's school has not been so accommodating. While it offers track as an option to its students both in the fall and spring, the runners do not use the facilities of a neighboring school or college; rather, they use the pathways around their campus buildings as a substitute for a track. Moreover, Jennifer's track coach has managed to book only a few competitions with other schools for the fall cross-country season and the spring. Jennifer's parents have asked a family friend to coach Jennifer in the 800 meters, using the facilities in public parks that are available to everyone.

During the past school year, Jennifer has trained with her private coach twice weekly. At school, the track coach supplements running around campus buildings with work in the gym. Inside the gym, the team usually goes through a number of interesting and valuable plyometric exercises. However, because Jennifer does not compete very often in dual meets or in regional championships, and despite working out under the private coach's direction, her time in the 800 meters over the past year has remained static. Her will to succeed is strong, but circumstances have continually cut into her best efforts.

On the other hand, Mark, who competes regularly, has improved dramatically in the 800. He is approaching a time of one minute fifty-five seconds as a junior. He attributes his progress mainly to very hard training and to the weekly competitions. Mark took it upon himself, in the fall, to add three early-morning half-hour fartlek-type runs, in addition to his regular late afternoon training sessions. Mark also understands that it is the all-out efforts of actual head-to-head competition that transforms the gains of smart and strenuous training into superior results. The main point here is that Mark, despite adversity, did what was necessary to achieve his goals. In a timely fashion, he solicited the help of administrators and coaches in order to be able to train and compete under favorable conditions. Jennifer, on the other hand, despite her winning spirit, never undertook the personal initiatives needed to train on a 400-meter track, nor did she talk to administrators and coaches about the possibility of competing more often. Jennifer has been forced to run around buildings and exercise indoors. Fortunately for Jennifer, she is about to enter her senior year. Her parents are at this time talking with the administration of her school to see whether the track team will be able to train at a local college track and adopt a regular competitive schedule. If these changes are not made, she will likely stagnate despite her growing physical strength and strong work ethic.

## Don't Make Assumptions

Never assume anything before a competition. While it's important to study your opponents in order to gain a competitive edge, never listen to gossip from teammates or opposing team members. Doing so can be self-defeating, crippling your chances before you even compete. Successful athletes stay flexible in their attitudes—watching their opponents carefully, but not succumbing to either extreme of defeatism or overconfidence.

The 2014 Iditarod (Alaska's 1,135-mile sled dog-race from Anchorage to Nome) featured terrible weather conditions. On the last day of the competition, the visibility was near zero due to blizzard-like winds and heavy snowfall. Dallas Seavey was two miles from the finish line, but knew he was in third place. Despite his position and the brutal conditions, Seavey continued to urge his tethered dog-team to finish strong. To lessen the burden on his dogs, Seavey decided to step off his sled and sprint the last two miles. Seavey's determination and ability to deal with pain paid off. Unbeknownst to him, he had passed the leaders at some point during the last minutes of the competition. It was only as he crossed the finish line that Seavey realized he was the 2014 Iditarod champion.

Seavey did not assume anything about the outcome of the race. Yes, he knew there were two obviously strong competitors ahead of him with two miles to go. However, Seavey made no sweeping deductions. His overriding thought was to go all out despite his exhaustion. His late-race heroism paid off handsomely.

Before important competitions, whatever the sport, you might hear or read all sorts of things regarding key participants and their chances of winning. You may be an unknown participant and assume you have no chance to win or place based on your past performances or on what others are saying. It is mind-boggling to realize how often the experts are wrong. It is for this reason that as a fearless competitor you should ignore what you cannot control and prepare for the competition at-hand fully focused on producing your confident, irrepressible best effort. A life-altering surprise may await you at the finish line or at the sound of the horn or buzzer!

Sometimes, athletes will try to "psych out" opponents by spreading false information about their own or their teammates' physical condition. Ignore this type of talk and focus on your own performance. Often, you will find that a competitor who has been much ballyhooed turns out not to be so invincible after all. Even the best competitors have off days, and you can be there at the top of your own game, ready to exploit the opportunity. The "unbeatable" athlete will not be expecting you to be such a formidable challenger. The "unbeatable" athlete will not be expecting the fearless storm you unleash.

This kind of dynamic upset was evident in a historic 1990 boxing match between Mike Tyson and Buster Douglas. The former was the undefeated heavyweight champion of the world with a record of 37 wins and no losses. Douglas was the betting underdog. Fortunately for Douglas, Tyson did not take the fight too seriously. Defending his title in the exotic city of Tokyo, Tyson indulged his fascination with Japan, soaking in the adulation and curiosity of the denizens of Japan's largest city. Meanwhile, Douglas was diligently training and single-mindedly rehearsing his and his handlers' battle plan: sharp jabs to keep Tyson's legendary, sometimes wild, inside attacks, including a devastating uppercut, out of range. As he approached the ring and entered it, Douglas appeared self-possessed and fearless. Though the fighters took turns dominating (Tyson occasionally connecting with his vaunted uppercut—in the eighth round he knocked Douglas down with it—and Douglas landing repeated jabs to keep Tyson at bay), the tide dramatically turned in Douglas's favor in round 10, as a barrage of powerful punches decked Tyson for the count.

The Tyson-Douglas bout fully illustrates the point we are making: Never assume that an individual opponent or team is invincible. It must be remembered that prior to the fight with Douglas, Tyson was universally considered one of the greatest heavyweights of all time.

## KEY TAKEAWAYS

- Never give up!
- Train your mind to remain composed when facing a formidable adversary.
- Never make assumptions or listen to pre-competition gossip.
- Never be intimidated by your adversary's reputation.

# 12

# The Psychology of Self-Discipline

*Self-discipline is the ability to do what you should do, when you should do it, whether you feel like it or not.*

—Elbert Hubbard

## LET US TAKE A REALISTIC LOOK

at the most useful psychological attribute an elite or ambitious athlete can possess: self-discipline, the ability to postpone gratification and take care of business first. This is the prime path to success in sports as well as in post-sports professional pursuits. Self-discipline leads to self-esteem and self-respect. It ensures that you will not be satisfied until your life's dreams are fulfilled. Without it, you are likely condemning yourself to a somewhat mediocre existence. Of course, there are exceptions, but on the whole, it is self-discipline that will be the key to your overall success in athletics and in life.

## The Disciplined Life

Self-disciplined athletes are the first to arrive on the field and the last to leave. They are the ones who spend hours watching videos of their games, as well as the games of their opponents, and taking notes; they are the ones the coach admires and saddles with responsibilities. The coach can count on these individuals to follow through. Moreover, self-discipline is portable. It can be effective on or off the field. Later, in the business world, for example, self-disciplined individuals rise inexorably to the top because they are willing to take on more responsibilities and organize their time to accommodate the extra challenges.

Yet self-discipline is a habit that only a relatively small percentage of society enjoys. These fortunate men and women possess the discipline-fueled drive to pursue their dreams in a sustained, well-organized, and energized fashion that leads to success. Let us take finances as an example. If you are self-disciplined, you will put a good portion of your liquid assets aside. The savings accumulate monthly and in fairly short order—as long as the monies in question are secure— you will be able to carefully invest part of your savings in a variety of long-term financial growth products, such as the best of the blue-chip stocks. Exercising self-discipline with your finances means postponing or avoiding frivolous purchases so that you can enjoy security in the long term—a comfortable retirement, college for your kids, and freedom from worry in your old age.

A self-disciplined life favorably affects your social relationships. Self-discipline provides the inner moral strength such that in time, you will recognize who in your social circle is worth cultivating as a true friend and who is not. When you possess a solid set of moral values you will not tolerate so-called friends who, in the final analysis, are untrustworthy and regularly flirt with trouble. When the news media reports on athletes who have gotten into some type of scrape, the infraction often occurs after midnight. While self-disciplined individuals are enjoying restful sleep, a number of their teammates are out "having a good time." Of course, being self-disciplined does not preclude you from being outgoing and fun-loving. On the contrary, the ambitious individual seeks self-actualization in many different spheres of daily life. That is part of the self-disciplined person's constant quest for personal improvement and for new knowledge. However, being socially and intellectually ambitious does not translate into taking unwise risks. Getting into late-night fights, abusing the opposite sex, drinking and driving, and so forth, do not reflect the values of the self-disciplined, aware athlete who is intent on self-improvement.

A life of discipline also requires a commitment to improving your mind. Many astute observers of professional sports in the U.S.A. bemoan the fact that few elite athletes spend time developing their intellect. Granted, professional athletes do stimulate their minds by memorizing the playbook or its equivalent, and by preparing for opponents during the competitive season. But what do most athletes do on the plane and bus on the way to a competition? They either sleep or listen to music. Reading material in the clubhouse or locker room is more or less limited to the sports pages. One exception who stands out for his self-discipline is Bill Bradley, formerly of the New York Knicks, who read book after book when travelling with the team. What we are saying here may smack of elitism on our part since Bradley attended Princeton University and was a Rhodes Scholar before becoming a professional basketball player. However, it is not meant to be elitist in any way. Our point is that disciplined athletes should be interested in steadily improving themselves as human beings, with all dimensions included: body, mind, heart, and soul. Thus, when retirement from the arena becomes a reality, they will be ready to apply self-discipline to a professional pursuit.

One athlete who turned his life around through self-discipline was Bernard Hopkins. Born in 1965, he grew up in the Raymond Rosen projects of North Philadelphia. He spent his time on the streets getting into fights and committing out-of-control acts of aggression. He was stabbed multiple times before the age of fourteen. His brother Michael was slain by a gunshot. Bernard continued to be a rough customer until his criminal activity got him sent to prison in 1982 at the age of seventeen. Though his sentence was projected to last eighteen years, Bernard was paroled in 1988.

His time in prison did not go to waste. In Pennsylvania's Gaterford State Penitentiary, a convicted murderer and former boxer named Michael "Smokey" Wilson introduced Hopkins to boxing. For the first time in his life, with the help of the three-time middleweight Pennsylvania penal-system champion, Wilson, Hopkins learned self-discipline. When, early on, Hopkins did not feel like training, Wilson would go fetch him and bring him to the practice ring. In time, Hopkins and Wilson formed a strong bond based on mutual admiration and respect. This relationship helped Hopkins to accomplish something many inmates have a difficult time doing: changing his basic self-image from a negative to a positive one.

Once paroled, Hopkins's determination to make something of himself in a world he had always viewed as hostile was immediately put to the test. He lost his first professional fight and spent sixteen months mulling over what his destiny would be: boxing or a return to the mean streets of Philadelphia. He ultimately made the decision to adhere to self-discipline, forge an iron will, and practice a new set of healthy values. Hopkins turned his back on drugs, alcohol, partying, and the rest. He desired to cleanse his mind and body of the debilitating habits that now repulsed him. For example, he began to shop for fresh, organic produce and to prepare meals himself. Part of this new approach to eating entailed no longer ingesting refined sugar, desserts, canned or processed food, caffeine, or tap water. His work ethic became legendary. Since Hopkins made an art of not being hit squarely in the ring, he was able to fight on Saturday night and return to the gym the very next Monday.

What's particularly remarkable is Hopkins's longevity in the sport. At the age of forty-nine in 2014, Hopkins held two of the four light-heavyweight World Championship titles (IBF and WBA). He also has attended well to his life outside the ring, including managing his money with security in mind. He preaches a basic financial philosophy: "Save your money." Hopkins is married with children. He sets a fine example for other fighters with regard to financial security, even though he has not attracted corporate advertising deals.

If you've ever wondered whether your personal background will enable you to achieve your dream of being an elite athlete, let Bernard Hopkins be one of your guides. He has been able to change his old ways and lead an exemplary life. The moral here is that no matter your background, no matter how you have comported yourself in the past, it is never too late to change for the better. Through self-discipline, you can work every day toward a better future.

## The Disciplined Athlete

In the realm of sports, self-discipline can make the difference between a good athlete and a great one. For example, the night before a competition, self-disciplined warriors will imagine how the upcoming contest will unfold and will take the time to visualize their positive role. For instance, Saul, a baseball pitcher, will visualize himself pitching to every batter he is likely to face the next day using the progression of pitches he feels are best suited for a positive outcome. Saul progresses through this visual rehearsal several times, affording himself the best mental preparation possible. Going through the opposing batting order repeatedly has the same effect on his central nervous system as having pitched several perfect games: no opposing player ever got out of the batter's box. The next day, during the actual game, Saul feels comfortable on the mound and supremely confident that he can throw hard-to-hit strikes and purposefully thrown non-strikes meant to keep the opposing batter off balance, unable to anticipate what type of pitch—fast ball, curve, slider, change-up, and so on—is coming and at what speed. Saul is well-prepared and in control because he had the self-discipline to mentally preview the upcoming game.

So, what is self-discipline? We have said earlier in this chapter that it is the ability to do something when you do not feel like doing it. In the realm of athletics, the finest example might be dressing and going to a workout when you feel like remaining in bed. Webster's dictionary defines it as "the correction or regulation of oneself for the sake of improvement," with the key words being "regulation" and "improvement." Regulation implies, for example, remaining calm under pressure and remaining at your functional best despite the challenges of your surrounding environment. Let us take, for instance, Madison Bumgarner's performance in game seven of the 2014 World Series. The immediate destiny of the San Francisco Giants was in his hands. When asked how he handled the pressure of such a situation, Bumgarner said he treated it like any other day. "Honestly, this might sound crazy, but I feel like when I'm out there pitching, I'm the same as I am standing here [at home in North Carolina] right now talking to you," he told *Sports Illustrated*. "I try to keep it that way. I try to be just like I am all the time." In Bumgarner's case, self-control means remaining himself—calmly confident and taking care of business in an optimally focused frame of mind.

If Bumgarner represents the "regulation" part of self-discipline, the other aspect—a continuous focus on improvement—is also vital. The most obvious form of improvement, within the context of this book, is the one regulated by hard, focused work in the competitive arena. In other words, you must be determined to improve and, thus, excel in your particular sport to the point of being consistently identified as an elite performer. The other constituent part of a drive for excellence has little to do with one's life in sports. It has everything to do with preparing for life after the last hurrah has sounded.

One athlete who embodies self-discipline is Olympic wrestler Dan Gable. Gable has been quoted as saying: "When I get tired working out and want to stop,

I wonder what my next opponent is doing. When I could 'see' him still working, I would start to push myself. You have to have a tough mind. If you know you have not cheated, physically, in your preparation, that makes you mentally tough." Gable's secret was knowing that his disciplined training ensured that he could produce his best till the last second of any match. In training, it was when he felt most exhausted that he would look for a fresh body to wrestle with. Even when Gable was in the off-season visiting his parents, he would make sure to bring a wrestler with him so that he could continue practice sessions in his home. He worked harder than anyone else; therefore, he had no problem believing in himself. Because of his outstanding discipline, Gable went on to world and Olympic championship titles.

In track coach Arthur Lydiard's book, *Running to the Top*, the author pinpoints twenty-one factors contributing to superior track performance. The sole psychological characteristic listed is self-discipline. As we have mentioned, self-discipline is the most important trait for success in any field, sport-related or not. Without it, it is unlikely that you will reach your full potential or attain elite sport status. The good news is that it takes only one moment of illuminating insight to begin travelling on the path of success fueled by self-discipline. Whatever your age or particular quest, you will benefit mightily from adherence to the principle of self-discipline. In the next chapter, we'll look at one of the best ways to cement your commitment to ongoing self-improvement in sports— which is, paradoxically, to fail.

## KEY TAKEAWAYS

- Self-discipline constitutes the most vital characteristic of successful individuals in general. It is the most important value of the athlete aspiring to elite sport status.

- Statistical studies indicate that self-discipline is the characteristic that best differentiates highly successful people from those who live paycheck to paycheck. Besides natural talent, self-discipline is the key value on which the aspiring athlete can ride on the path to elite stardom.

- Self-discipline leads to self-respect and self-confidence. When athletes know that they have done their very best to prepare for the competitive season, they exude composure and the will to win.

# 13

# Dealing with Failure

*Failures teach us resolve to overcome. [...] At best our failures
provide us with an enemy to conquer. That enemy is mostly ourselves.
In learning to prevail over weaknesses the greatest
human achievements have been made.*

—David Viscott, M.D.

## ASK YOUR PARENTS HOW MANY TIMES

you fell down before you learned how to walk or ride a bike on your own. Even
though you fell down, your parents kept standing you up and, before too long,
you were running and biking independently. Essentially, you worked through
many failed attempts before you became fully successful.

Learning from failure is a critical element that separates the elite athlete from
others who give up easily or succumb to a defeatist mentality. It's certain that you
will experience failure as an athlete; the only uncertainty is how you will cope
with it. How you deal with failure tells a lot about what kind of person, athlete,
or coach you will be. The greatest men and women in history all learned from
failure and moved on to success. In this chapter, we'll learn two key strategies
that helped them along the way.

## Stay Calm and Don't Wallow

The first thing you need to decide right now is that when failure and defeat happen—which they will, to one degree or another—you are not going to allow yourself to wallow in disappointment. Do not sit around feeling sorry for yourself after a defeat; this will only put you behind in reaching your goal of becoming great.

Giving in to defeat can be a vicious cycle. When you experience an emotional sting after a loss, you might start to imagine that you're a lousy athlete and that you don't have a future in your sport. Then you might take it one step further, convincing yourself that since you are a poor athlete with no chance of winning, there's really no point in continuing to practice. Before you know it, you might actually *become* that lousy athlete unable to achieve success—not because it started out being true, but because you made it a self-fulfilling prophecy by allowing an emotional defeat to deter you from working that much harder to become the athlete you wanted to be. You surrendered to your disappointment and fear.

Be inspired instead by the example of Meredith Kessler, a triathlete who has known plenty of disappointments. During a full triathlon, she was passed at mile ten of the marathon leg and figured her chances of winning were shattered. Being passed by someone who set an "amazing pace," she says, was a "mentally crushing and a potentially debilitating event." But rather than succumbing to her disappointment during the race, she drew strength from her reliable motto for keeping emotions in check. "I try to remember KCCO (keep calm and carry on) all race long," she says. And Kessler found to her surprise that by mile twelve, her opponent had slowed and Kessler was able to catch up. Kessler attributes her eventual win to her decision to not give up during that moment of despair. She remained composed and maintained her pace.

In the context of remaining calm under pressure, we can appreciate the life of Les Stroud, the "survivorman" who has spent a decade in the Canadian wilderness. The advice he gives to anyone who needs to survive a dangerous situation is always the same: "The very first thing is you must calm down. It doesn't matter what the circumstances are. Only then can you think clearly to find a way out of those circumstances." In difficult moments, you don't have the luxury of giving in to fear, disappointment, or anger. You have a job to do.

If you are part of a losing effort as a team member, you can stand out by refusing to give up. Till the final whistle blows, you can stay motivated and focused on doing your job well in the face of adversity. When the coach goes back over the videos of the contest, he or she will notice how you performed from the first to the last moments. You never gave in; your spirit remained undaunted.

One attitude worth emulating is that of the French swimmer Yannick Agnel, the 2014 world and 2012 Olympic 200-meter freestyle swimming champion. In most of his interviews, Agnel stresses the fun aspect of his training. Though he admits to harboring a revulsion for losing, he enters into all competitions, whether he is tired or not, with the following strategy: Go all-out from the sound of the horn and do not allow any disruptive thought to enter the mind. Knowing he has trained to the maximum of his ability allows Agnel to remain loose throughout his races. However, were the occasional loss he encountered early in his career to repeat itself, it would only provide an incentive to rethink his training strategies and to remain confident, focused, and loose in subsequent competitions.

Like your parents taught you when you learned to walk, and ride a bike, the best thing you can do after a failure is pick yourself up and focus on your goal once again. Don't let your emotions get the better of you. For example, at the very end of his undefeated college wrestling career, Dan Gable lost to an individual named Larry Owens. Gable cried and took it hard. However, he began immediately to work harder than ever, and went on to win Olympic gold. This is an excellent example for you to follow. It's normal to feel disappointment after a defeat or failure, but giving in to fear or an occasional lack of confidence may lead you to become afraid of trying new things. It may prevent you from pursuing your dreams.

## Learn from Your Mistakes

Along with controlling your emotions, a second key way to deal with failure is to always use your mistakes as tools in your ongoing improvement as an athlete. Get right back up and learn from defeat. Move on with a fixation on improving yourself. Master mind-control in order to self-talk and visualize your way through failure. It takes daily practice to achieve this type of self-mastery, but it can be done. When you think you've got it down, practice some more. Read or memorize self-talk scripts that help provide the impetus toward a healthy attitude in defeat. Say to yourself, for instance, "I recognize my mistake. I do not feel any shame. I have learned an important lesson. When faced with an identical or similar situation in the future, I will do the right thing. In the meantime I will continue to visualize myself performing in a winning manner."

Learning from mistakes is what elite athletes do. According to MMA fighter Renzo Gracie, failure is a necessary part of the process. "There are fights when everything seemed lost and I won," he explains. "I always tell my students that the loss is where you can get better. Once you make a mistake in a fight or a competition, you 'never do that again.' It's burned in your brain. . . . You only fail by not learning."

So according to Gracie, the only real failure is if you don't learn from your mistakes. Decide right now that you are going to learn from adversity, and that you will also listen to constructive criticism that is aimed at improving your performance. One athlete who allowed constructive criticism to make him better than anyone else is former basketball star Michael Jordan. While it's true that Jordan was born with unusual talents, his famous moves on the court did not come naturally to him. In high school, in fact, he did not immediately make the varsity team. When he asked the coach to provide a reason, the coach indicated that Jordan's foul shooting was weak. From that day forward, for ten straight years, Jordan did not go to bed without having made five hundred foul shots. He went on to have a legendary professional basketball career, including an outstanding record related to free throw percentage. Again, good things come from a strong work ethic that is far superior to the norm, and from an ability to learn from mistakes and weaknesses.

Reality dictates that, especially initially, you may fail occasionally, so you had better learn how to deal with it. Learning from failure is not always easy, but it can happen. We enjoy reading books about people who started from the bottom and have worked their way up and succeeded. Movies such as *Rocky* encourage viewers to keep pushing forward. There are probably more inspirational quotes about overcoming failure than any other subject. Babe Ruth and many other sports legends have admitted to failing quite often before they succeeded on a regular basis. Even Thomas Edison, the greatest inventor of all time, talked about the number of prototypes that didn't work before he invented the light bulb.

The following is a personal anecdote that illustrates the meaning of "the agony of defeat" and how to deal with it. The 2005 and 2006 Division I NCAA wrestling champion at 165 lbs. was Oklahoma State's Johnny Hendricks. In 2007, I (Dan Valahu) attended the national tournament in Saint Louis, Missouri, where Hendricks reached the finals again, but lost a tightly contested match. The next morning at the airport, I found myself sitting a few yards from Hendricks and several of his teammates. A deeply inconsolable sadness was etched on his face. I now regret not having approached him to utter a few hopefully consoling words. Moreover, had I been a close friend of his, I would have urged him to return to Oklahoma State University with a stoic attitude, his head held high, the posture of a two-time national champion, and the 2007 runner-up. Not an easy thing to do, but the sooner you learn from a mistake, and begin to look forward, the better.

## KEY TAKEAWAYS

- Regardless of the adverse situation, continue to go all out in your efforts to succeed.

- Use mind control to avoid panic-like symptoms or a defeatist attitude when a competition is not going well. Calm down; reflect on ways to dig yourself or your team out of trouble.

- Learn from your mistakes, but do not dwell on them. Once you have examined the mistake with a clear mind, forget about it or do what is necessary to correct it.

# 14

# Dealing with Success

*Self-reliance is initiative. You must start with initiative, keep initiative and end with initiative. Your welfare is your own at all times. If you do give up your initiative, you have no one to blame except yourself.*

—Willard and Marguerite Beecher

**SOMETIMES, DEALING WITH ATHLETIC SUCCESS** is actually as hard as dealing with failure. You may be surprised to learn that you have to be as careful and deliberate about assimilating success into your life as you are about moving forward from failure. You don't want your success to become a destructive force. Such was the case with golfer Tiger Woods.

At the high point of his career, Woods went off the deep end. Once he did, his ability to concentrate on the golf course seemed affected. How did this happen? The answer is not too hard to fathom. Before the scandal involving multiple girlfriends and the ensuing divorce, Woods felt invincible. He had good reason to feel that way. His success on the links at a young age engendered adulation, money, and self-confidence. As can happen to people with power who are in the limelight, Woods apparently became attracted to the thrill of leading a secret double life. Supremely confident as he was on the golf course, he must have felt that he could handle flirting with trouble. In time, his relationships derailed his marriage and led to devastating public awareness of behavior that both shocked and titillated the public.

Though Woods may have initially thought the scandal would blow over and he would return to glory on the links, something psychological may have occurred that he did not have the maturity to deal with. A debilitating thought may have crept into his mind, one that to this day may be crippling his game, preventing Woods from excelling in his usual manner. The thought? The knowledge that the entire universe now identifies Woods as a failed human being, one who tried to hide a lifestyle that his fans would not appreciate and which strongly contradicted the image Woods so gracefully projected. This knowledge may have lodged itself in Woods's psyche and upset his ability to concentrate fully on attaining perfection on the links as he once was able to do. Without doubt, Woods has learned from his mistakes, and likely is espousing the right values. However, he has not yet managed to bring his game back to a level of excellence that inspired so many people. In this chapter we'll highlight some strategies to keep you from making troublesome mistakes that arise from an inability to deal with success in a healthy manner.

## Maintaining Your Integrity

No matter what level of athletic success you have attained, whether it's leading your high school team to the finals at Regionals or being drafted by an NBA team, one possible consequence is known as the "Big Head." This psychological state leads to a loss of focus with regard to reaching ultimate goals. You may begin to be selfish as a player, worrying only about stats and money. You might start imagining that you are a star and are far better than all your teammates or competitors.

Success should encourage you to remain focused and continue to strive to better yourself by working hard. You have to decide ahead of time that you are going to maintain your integrity and not let your ego become inflated.

Those individuals who gain fame in college or the professional ranks should think twice before changing their values and the training habits that led to fame. On the professional level many first-round draft choices never amount to much and eventually retire prematurely. You may never reach the professional ranks, but you can learn from those athletes' inability to handle their own success.

What causes some athletes to underperform? Did their success affect their psyche or modify their work ethic? At times, the reason for under-achievement has to do with a new environment and new coach. Whatever the problem, the athlete in question must find the way and get help to deal with success gone wrong.

It is paramount for you as an outstanding athlete to concentrate on training and doing what is necessary to improve, thereby solidifying the position you have attained. It is fine to go out with friends or teammates to unwind; however, it is of the utmost importance to take care of team business first. Take any complimentary remarks other people may be voicing about you in stride by working daily to improve your already-established skills. Don't let the hype go to your head. Also, steer clear of trouble. Success can slip through your hands very easily in today's world of twenty-four hour news, sport channels, cell-phone cameras, and social media posts. Particularly because you are successful on the field, court, pool, etc., it behooves you to stay far away from potential trouble. Success on the college and professional level attracts myriad individuals who will desire your company and flatter you, but who do not have your best interests at heart. Be smart and in control of your daily actions in order to avoid problematic situations. Remain close to family and long-time true friends.

In the event you feel that you are experiencing trouble sticking to the straight and narrow, seek immediate help from a wise, trusted friend, coach, counselor, or family member. Though in your mind you may believe that you can get away with unwise behavior, chances are that sooner rather than later the police or school authorities will catch up with you. Don't throw your athletic future away because of ingrained, detrimental behavior; be smart. Seek the healthy, safe environment that will allow you to concentrate on working on your athletic gifts rather than finding yourself unable to join your teammates because of suspension or worse. Think it over. What was it that brought you attention and fame in the first place? And as mentioned above, choose now as the moment you will change your risky ways.

## Continue Working Hard

Another potential pitfall of success is that you may lose your motivation. If you've already met your goals or had a successful athletic season, why not take it easy for a while? After a hard competitive few months, you will just want to relax. A period of relaxation is necessary, of course. When it's time to hit the gym or the pool, however, your friends and family may want you to hang out, and it will be difficult to tell them you can't. Then, nutrition problems may materialize; you may start going out to clubs where you drink alcohol and eat unhealthy food late at night. You may even be confronted by an aggressive individual who wants trouble. Do and say all you can to avoid a serious confrontation. Tell the aggressor that you agree with him or her and are sorry to have created a problem. Of course, even if the evening goes well, there are consequences. You get to bed quite late, throwing off your daytime routine. Upon rising, you feel sluggish; the last thing you want to do is work out. Before you know it, you are overweight and have lost all motivation to hit the gym, pool, or playing field. This is how you begin to fall behind and how you become less than average, leading to a short career. We see this materialize all the time.

So, how do you stop this syndrome from occurring? Begin preparing your mind before the season ends. Then, following a restorative break, begin working on getting stronger and faster, becoming leaner while putting on more muscle. It's hard to do this during the season because the competitive schedule may not permit it. In the off-season, you will want to research reading materials, and talk to trainers and coaches as you establish a program designed to propel you to a higher level of mastery in your sport. The reality is that most elite athletes use innovation in the off-season to improve their skills. Do not be part of the minority of great athletes who feel it is time to take it easy in the off-season and consequently lose their edge.

Start the off-season training cycle by sending an email to friends and family telling them about your goals and your commitment to be the best you can be. Explain that you need them to be there for you. Family and close friends can help you stay focused and avoid distractions. They can help make sure that you are eating correctly. Let them know how much you appreciate their sacrifice and thoughtfulness. This will take a lot of pressure off you. However, while some people will help, others will tempt you. This is when you must determine what is more important: to improve or regress. You will have to make a choice and then live with it.

The off-season can also be a great time for you to rediscover your love for your chosen sport. Above all, your passion is the best way to stay motivated and continue working hard. When you play for the love of the game it's not in your makeup to dampen your commitment; you always give it all you have. For instance, if your team is down by twenty or winning by twenty you continue to hustle all the way until the final whistle blows or the buzzer sounds. When you stand out among the rest in adverse situations, you will get noticed. It is this that will lead you to having the status of a leader and eventually a legend. Play for the love of the game. Of course, if you are hurt during competition (concussion, pull, strain, and the like), be sure to put yourself immediately in the trainer's and doctor's hands.

In conclusion, ask yourself if there is a hidden part of you that could eventually derail your career. Don't fall victim to your own success, becoming your own worst enemy. If alcohol or drugs are part of your existence, now is the time to take control of your life and future. If you need help, find it. If this entails rehab, do not feel ashamed. Do the right thing. In case your problem is psychological in nature, good therapists and effective medicine are one initiative away.

## KEY TAKEAWAYS

- Bad habits may come with professional success. Maintain your integrity and don't succumb to an inflated ego.
- Avoid late night outings or celebrations. Likewise, avoid belligerent individuals, particularly if they have had too much to drink.
- As will be expounded on later, seek immediate help for serious addictions.
- Do what is needed, particularly in the off-season, to raise your game. Never be satisfied with your present condition.

# PART 4

# PERSONAL BEHAVIOR AND TEAMMATE RELATIONSHIPS

# 15

# Relationships and Personal Conduct

*If we are to be happy and successful we must have . . . regard for others . . . remembering that we are part of the human family. We must respect the dignity of others, the fact that every person is a child of God. We must take the trouble to think of other people's feelings and viewpoints, their desires and needs. We must act as if other people are important and treat them accordingly . . . and when necessary, help them.*

—Maxwell Maltz, M.D.

## THE PERSON WHO COMES TO OUR MIND

when we think of a kind, thoughtful, and generous athlete is Missy Franklin (Melissa Jeanette Franklin) of world backstroke swim fame. Why Franklin? She treats people from all walks of life in a warm, unassuming manner. Instead of cashing in on her multiple Olympic medals and world-record success, Franklin chose to remain an amateur so that she could attend college at the University of California, Berkeley. Rather than exploiting her increased fame, Franklin has chosen to become a philanthropist of sorts. Her charitable pursuits include the Swim for Multiple Sclerosis, One Drop USA (a clean water project), and speaking to various civic groups. Franklin represents the best our society has to offer. She is not only an athlete; she is also a human being with an altruistic soul.

Like Missy Franklin, it is possible for successful athletes to demonstrate as much leadership in their relationships and personal interactions as they do in their chosen sport. This chapter deals primarily with how elite athletes can enjoy harmonious relationships with team members and other important people in their lives, and the personal habits that make for a successful life.

## Practicing Kindness to All

Elite athletes who are successful in sports and in life know that there exists one prime ingredient for success: practicing kindness to all people. And by "all" we do mean all: Every person you encounter is worthy of your respect. This broader message of brotherhood and sisterhood is beautifully expressed by Joshua Liebman in his book *Peace of Mind*: "The humble virtue of simple kindness . . . is good to contemplate in our daily lives," he reminds us. "We cannot afford to forget that the superb charter of kindliness includes salespersons, our own domestic help, the garage mechanic, and the tailor who presses our clothes. Too many of us deal in high-sounding platitudes about the 'brotherhood of man [and woman],' but exhibit an ugly class consciousness by treating the janitor as though he belonged to an inferior breed." You are not inherently superior to anyone else if you are an athlete, or you are smart, or your family has money. You don't have the right to look down upon others or treat them poorly. As Liebman puts it, human relationships "will work better when we take the time, patience, and love to discover what our fellow beings look like, to learn their names, and to regard them as human beings." This message of tolerance and love certainly applies to all of us, including elite athletes and their world.

Let us talk a moment about the types of relationships that can be formed among players on large teams (swimming, wrestling, soccer, baseball, and football, to name just a few). Ideally, team chemistry evolves in such a way that most athletes on a squad get along well with the vast majority of their teammates. As team members, each works to understand, trust, respect, and help everyone else. Within this ideal situation, however, players also tend to form little groups inside the larger ones, based on natural affinities, be they psychological, moral, cultural, athletic, and so on. Whatever the interrelational patterns, be sure to take initiatives to get to know, or at least to say kind words, to those teammates who participate little or not at all in competitive encounters. Above all, make the effort to understand and help them.

The ideal world we just painted is not always attainable. When it is somewhat tarnished by one or more conflicts, tolerance should be the first impulse; that is, tolerance in the sense of restraint. Tolerance is a sign of maturity. In practical terms it means not reacting reflexively when aggressive impulses take hold of the mind and emotions. Of course, there exist situations when an immediate response is necessary because a teammate has gone way too far with words or actions and deserves some form of reprimand. However, in the majority of cases, the wisest option is initial silence and reflection. When a fan or onlooker says or does something crass to you, use mind control to ignore the insult. On the very rare occasions in his life when someone confronted the author, David Hill, he immediately defused the confrontation by telling the aggressor that he was a family man and wanted no part of a fight.

When first meeting teammates, tolerance means avoiding snap judgments while accepting all individuals as they are. If you have reason to censure an individual, let the captain or an especially even-tempered and respected teammate intercede by talking calmly with the person whose actions or words are out of line.

If you are a junior or senior, or if you are a veteran at your game, resist being abusive to younger players. You may be thinking that there is a certain individual whose behavior gets under your skin. Well, do you recall the early chapters in this book whose theme was mind control? Just as you have trained your mind to remain positive and focused when the referee makes a bad call or when the coach puts you on the bench, you can also maintain an aggression-free, positive frame of mind when exposed to a difficult teammate. When I (David Hill) was training for a sixth consecutive international kickboxing title (WKA/1993), a young fighter from Dallas stopped by our club for a workout. My trainer suggested that our guest and I go through a series of offensive and defensive moves. Midway through the exercise, the young guest stung me with a kick to the head, only partially blocked by me. I complained to my trainer. When I look back on the incident, I realize that the young up-and-coming fighter was simply attempting to do his part of the two-man exercise as well as he could. I now admit to myself that my accidental training partner meant no harm. Though lighter and less experienced than I, he was extremely limber and was able to deliver the kick in question with unexpected speed. I should have congratulated him instead of complaining.

Adopt a considerate, open-minded attitude with people you encounter. Even if teammates appear to be grumpy or disagreeable, greet them with a smile and a warm hello. If you treat individuals the way you wish to be treated, rewards are usually forthcoming. Never underestimate or overestimate new people you meet. Remain open-minded enough to allow the relationship to develop naturally. Among teammates, this approach is especially important. A band of athletes who respect each other's individuality will experience visible rewards during training and competitions. Remember: When the final whistle blows, be conscious of the pain experienced by the losers. If you are defeated, be gracious to the winners.

Elsewhere in this volume, we have mentioned the currently-in-vogue concept of "mindfulness." As applied to sports in general, remember that teammates or individuals you meet who practice your sport may come from parts of the United States with which you are not familiar. These individuals may hold opinions that are different from yours. Mindfulness (focused yet relaxed in-the-moment reflection/visualization in a quiet, soft-lit environment) at once solves problems of a practical or psychological nature. It also functions well in a context more aligned with human relations. If you are exposed to individuals on your team with whom you do not get along, allow mindful meditation to neutralize and transform your tolerance and suspicion-based intuitions into forgiveness, compassion, and selflessness. In case you are wondering, transformative meditation, as it relates to human interactions, does not make you a weak person; it liberates you to focus on solutions in any and all stressful situations. If others do not reciprocate in kind, you are free to alter relations to a smile and courteous "hello."

## Dealing with Depression and Avoiding Abusive Behavior

As an outstanding athlete, part of your commitment to excellence in sports and life will be a pledge to maintain good mental health. Depression can affect athletes at all levels and all sporting endeavors, perhaps even more than the general population. An NCAA report on depression and college sports stated that 18 percent of U.S. adults suffer from some kind of mental disorder, and that college is a particularly difficult time because of increased stress, anxiety about high expectations, and a lack of sleep. College athletes "are known to encounter unique stressors that the general population doesn't have to deal with, such as time demands, relationships with coaches, and missed scheduled classes," the report said. Athletes face all of the demands of college *and* all of the demands of elite sports, which include weekdays spent studying and practicing their sport and weekends traveling for away games, disrupting sleep patterns and contributing to overall stress levels. Moreover, they are noticeably less likely to seek professional help than non-athletes, which means they may be trying to deal with their psychological burdens all alone.

Athletes may have an additional vulnerability if they have suffered traumatic brain injuries in the course of their athletic careers. Ted Johnson, a linebacker for ten seasons with the New England Patriots incurred more than one hundred concussions on the field. The book *Brain: The Complete Mind* states that after retiring in 2005, Johnson "fell into a deep depression, which he believes may have been caused by his chronic concussions." Recent studies by the Boston University School of Medicine reveal the long-term damage-potential caused by injuries to the brain. "Neuroscientists analyzed [ ... ] the brains of several athletes, including Andre Waters, the onetime National Football League player whose deep depression and ultimate suicide at age 44 have been linked to chronic concussions. Waters' brain, the study found, bore microscopic protein tangles much like those of Alzheimer's patients nearly twice his age."

Depression afflicts female athletes just as it does male competitors. The golf great Christina Kim, already subject to depression, became so despondent upon hearing about the suicide of Robin Williams (the actor-comedian who died in 2014) that she came very close to plunging from a balcony to her death. After this episode, she confided the worst of her depressive symptoms to her best friends, fellow tour players Michelle Wie, Jane Park, and Irene Cho. These friends, and a prescription for antidepressants, saved her life. Once she had received help, Kim went on to her first North American victory in nine years, at the Lorena Ochoa Invitational in Mexico City.

Kim's story demonstrates that a combination of talk therapy and medicine is quite effective in bringing all types of depression under control. Yet many people are reluctant to seek treatment—perhaps especially athletes, who want to be perceived as strong and always in control. But if depression affects you, it is not something to be ashamed of. Know that a doctor who specializes in prescribing medicine for depression and related conditions is today equipped to find the best pharmacological solution for you. Show how courageous and smart you are by seeking help and taking care of such business as early as possible. The earlier in your life that psychological problems are discussed with a professional, the better the outcome. Take the time to talk confidentially to a psychologist or psychiatrist (the latter can prescribe medication) about problems that are now hidden but can be neutralized and brought under control with medicine and with one-on-one conversations with a counselor.

As you promote your mental wellness by seeking professional help when necessary, it's also vital to avoid abusive situations. Conflicts between spouses and partners are largely inevitable; however, the same mind control and self-talk mechanisms that work on the field and court can be applied when you're experiencing anger or similar negative emotions. Strong emotions are difficult to control. That is a given. Aggressive behavior may be triggered by jealousy, insecurity, immaturity, undiagnosed bipolarity, or some combination of such. Only the habit-forming, repeated use of mind control and self-talk will impede regrettable action when a major conflict arises. So, make the self-talk mechanisms you learned in Part I constants of your daily life. In this way, you stand a much better chance of demonstrating restraint when strong emotions are about to take control. You will be better able to handle unexpected or challenging situations as they arise, as they regularly do. When something occurs that taxes your ability to react with the proper restraint, remember to remain calm until you can gather yourself to implement the mind control and self-talk mechanisms you know so well. If by chance you find yourself reverting to the "old" ways of behaving, do not be hard on yourself. Don't let disappointment linger; just turn things around and learn from the experience.

Sadly, many athletes never learn this kind of self-control, and may resort to bullying and physical abuse. Some schools are taking this problem seriously and implementing change throughout their sports programs. School officials in Sayerville, N.J. cancelled the remaining football games of its team over "allegations of bullying, intimidation and harassment among players." And at the University of Texas, a groundbreaking program that is the first of its kind aims "to aid character development in young athletes [at both the college and high-school levels] to help them be positive role models." The new UT Center for Sports Leadership and Innovation helps coaches and mentors intervene to curb troubling behavior or violent tendencies among athletes. The article goes on to cite Texas football coach Charlie Strong's core values for his team: "honesty, treating women with respect, no stealing, no guns and no drugs."

## Avoiding Drugs and Alcohol

Coach Strong was right to say that drugs have no place among the core values needed to be successful in sports. But substance abuse is all too common. For example, athletes who are suffering from stress or anxiety may turn to alcohol consumption to ease their debilitating condition. Carousing at a favorite bar with teammates can become a habit. The end result may be a DWI conviction and the life-altering consequences that follow: possible jail time, heavy fines, and an unwanted addition to one's permanent record.

Of late, newspapers and television news are replete with stories chronicling physical abuse, sexual battery, late night fights, fraternity binge drinking, and the like. More and more women are accusing college administrators of turning a blind eye to accusations of rape committed by well-known athletes. The latter often manage to escape any substantive punishment.

Do the following when tempted to use physical force in an inappropriate way. First, stop, breathe deeply, and reflect before allowing a strong emotion to dictate how you are going to act. Second, think before speaking or acting in a provocative manner. Third, manage to stay away from so-called friends whose behavior and habits are dangerous and/or illegal. Now is the time to reconsider any behavior on your part that can propel you into a danger zone. Michael Phelps, for one, has made a few missteps, but he has decided that enough immature behavior is enough. We are not saying that going out with friends is not a good idea. On the contrary, good friendships are important, the key to a long, enjoyable life. They reduce stress and add stability and happiness to one's existence. The wrong friends and late-night sorties are the problem. They can lead to abusive behavior of various stripes.

Substance abuse can't be dismissed as a normal part of the party scene. In many cases, people who become dependent on alcohol or drugs do so because they are self-medicating for undiagnosed mental health conditions. Stress at work, school, or on the field can cause them to look for quick but dangerous solutions. In the long run, drugs and alcohol are detrimental to their health and can actually have an effect opposite to the intended release from stress, bringing even more anxiety and emotional upheaval into their lives. As we have seen, it is better to learn healthy coping mechanisms to deal with competition-related anxiety. If this situation describes you, seek confidential help before it is too late. As we have seen, there exist medicines and therapies that are very effective in treating substance abuse and anxiety disorders. Be courageous and seek out appropriate options.

Another kind of drug abuse prevalent in sports is the use of drugs not for recreation or self-medication, but to improve athletic performance. In the modern era, as was the case in Ancient Greece, athletes at all levels of competition have turned to performance-enhancing drugs and dietary supplements to improve strength, speed, and stamina and "to get the edge" on their competitors. In *When Winning Costs Too Much: Steroids, Supplements and Scandal in Today's Sports* (2006), John McClaskey and Julian Bailes reveal that a minimum of 24 percent of high school, college, and pro football players are doping, and with regard to supplements, "44 percent of twelfth-grade male athletes in a suburb of New York reported using creatine." Despite the horrific consequences of consuming performance-enhancing drugs, the modern era has been witness to a series of an ever-more sophisticated line of products that began to surface in the late 1960s with steroids. According to McClaskey and Bailes, long-term steroid use can cause serious health problems related to "heart, liver, serum lipids, reproductive function, atherosclerosis, the immune system, and the psyche."

Anabolic steroids, which create a synthetic version of testosterone, are known to build muscle and are sometimes legitimately prescribed to people whose muscles have atrophied due to injury or illness. But as Brian Chichester and Jack Croft point out in *Powerfully Fit*, these drugs can be quite dangerous if used by otherwise healthy athletes. "Unfortunately, thanks to a black market and blind ambition, steroids are used by some bodybuilders and other athletes wanting to build muscle fast," they write. "Abusing steroids [ ... ] can put your physical and mental health at risk. Abusers can experience drastic mood swings, including depression or uncontrolled aggression [ ... ], extreme acne, impotence, rashes and, in the long term, heart disease, liver tumors and testicle shrinkage. Sometimes they die."

Despite such health risks, drug producers have created ever-more sophisticated products over the past forty years: beta-2 agonist drugs, human growth hormone (GH), EPO, diuretics, amphetamines, THG and PEDS, to name some of the most used but banned performance-enhancing products. It's not only male athletes who employ them, though research suggests that men are more than three times as likely to do so as women. Some top female athletes, such as the runners Marion Jones and Kelli White, have been implicated in doping scandals—in Jones's case, at the cost of her Olympic gold medal. The NFL, NBA, and the Olympic Committee, among other governing bodies, monitor drug use and have substance abuse policies that all athletes and teams must follow. These policies are enforced by the leagues, the coaches, and in some cases, by international doping committees. Unfortunately, newspapers have been full of articles outlining tendencies by certain governing agencies to overlook positive testing results for various reasons, all illegal.

It's vital that the athlete who aspires to improve or reach elite status avoid becoming dependent upon performance-enhancing drugs. Likewise, it's paramount that you handle any stress or emotional challenges you may face through healthy coping mechanisms, and not drugs or alcohol. If you possess a superior work ethic and a warrior-like attitude, you do not need to abuse prescription or illicit drugs in order to cope with adversity and anxiety.

## KEY TAKEAWAYS

- Open-minded tolerance is the sign of maturity. Avoid making snap judgments when meeting people for the first time. Try to accept individuals as they are.

- If, as an athlete, you infringe on team rules, go directly to your coach to explain the situation. If you break the law, go to the police. Never hide the truth.

- Develop a strong set of moral values. If you are in a position of authority, let athletes know that unwise or criminal behavior will not be tolerated.

- Avoid becoming dependent upon alcohol, recreational drugs, or performance-enhancing drugs. The long-term consequences to your health and life are not worth any short-term relief or results these substances may provide.

- In case of depression, remember that a psychiatrist can prescribe medicine and a psychologist can talk you through your particular problems.

# 16

# Becoming a Team Leader

*One for all, and all for one.*

—Alexandre Dumas

**WHEN I (DAN VALAHU) WAS IN HIGH SCHOOL,** our football team was part of a league that included a perennial archrival. In our senior year, our coach, who sent in plays via a shuttle system, never called a pass play involving our best player during the game that preceded the most important game of the season. We won the game easily, but our pass-catching phenomenon moaned and groaned during half-time and post-game. He was inordinately upset. Only much later did he learn that our coach had not included him in the play calling so that scouts in the stands would not see the plays that included our pass-catching wizard. Our star player went on to become all-City and all-State. However, no one on the team forgot his moaning and groaning. Certainly, his immature display was characteristic of selfishness as opposed to being a team player who was ready to sacrifice for the overall good of the team.

There are many athletes who desire to become team leaders. However, are they ready and do they really want the responsibility? Being a team leader is not an easy task. You have to be willing to inspire by example.

## Put the Team First

It has been said that effective teamwork divides the task and multiplies the success. The ideal is to have everyone working together as one. With this mindset, the word "team" stands for

- Together

- Everyone

- Achieves

- More

If you are a team player, you commit yourself to doing your best with passion, regardless of game-day strategic planning which may diminish your individual role for the sake of victory. Be mature; do not worry about how many times you touch the ball in any particular contest. Your time will come, particularly if the coach sees how well you carry out your role.

Becoming a team leader begins with earning the respect of players and coaches. Respect comes from leading. For example, how can you ask someone else to do something when you're not willing to do it yourself? Notice we use the word "ask" instead of "tell" or "order." When you tell someone to do something, you are going to have problems and, in time, will lose authority. No one likes being told what to do. On the other hand, if you ask politely and propose thoughtful choices, you will make teammates feel as if they have a say in the matter and are to some degree in control.

As a leader you should keep your word. If you tell someone you are going to do something and you do not do it, then respect may be lost. Most importantly, a team leader must earn trust. Team members have to believe that the leader cares about them as individuals and has their best interest at heart. If you are a team leader, you need to be aware of the individual needs of your teammates. If a player is having trouble with allergies, for example, don't hesitate to accompany him or her to the appropriate health practitioner with the coach's blessing. Thus, a leader not only takes initiatives during competition but is aware of problems concerning teammates during practice and in the off-season.

A leader must learn how to interact with a wide range of personalities and show empathy for all teammates. Each individual has a unique personality and manner of accepting situations. Strive to know your teammates personally. Some of them may possess problematic personalities; work to get along with them. When you see them, smile. When you encounter a difficult conflict, stay calm and do not let yourself lose control. When you notice that small groups of athletes tend to isolate themselves from the rest of the team, go over to them as a friend and mingle, with sincere freindships as the motivation.

Learn how to give a great motivational speech in front of the team before or during a competitive event. Look up and memorize quotes from great coaches and players to be used as motivational tools when giving a talk. Know when to lower and raise your voice. Show confidence with your body language when you speak, and always speak from the heart. Take the initiative to schedule team meetings, with or without coaches present, during which anyone can express ideas, grievances, and ways to make the team function better. Consequently, everyone feels they are being heard from in a manner that prevents hidden locker-room dissension. Moreover, such meetings, the context of which remains confidential, serve to unify the team and enhance team spirit and loyalty.

With the coach's blessing, as a team leader, you can arrange to show a particularly moving and inspirational film or documentary that the entire team watches, following performance-related comments from the coach. What an original way to start an important week of practice. For the critical competition to follow, you and the coach can arrange for recently graduated star players to visit the locker room. It is sometimes these simple initiatives that distinguish one team's collective spirit from another.

## Resolve Conflict Appropriately

What if one or two individuals on a team are clearly anti-social, or upset with the way they are being treated by the coaching staff? Well, instead of being locked into a confrontational situation, the head coach, staff, and team leader should collectively search for ways to defuse the situation rather than letting it fester. The head coach, for example, could set up a one-on-one meeting with the player(s) in question, during which grievances are aired and solutions are sought.

When you are leading a team, it's vital to learn to resolve conflict in a healthy way. One of the wisest of ancient philosophers, Marcus Aurelius, commented on just such a situation:

> Begin the morning by saying to yourself, I shall meet with the busybody, the ungrateful, arrogant, deceitful, envious, unsocial. [ ... ] I can neither be injured by any of them, for no one can fix on me what is ugly, nor can I be angry with my kinsman, nor hate him. For we are made for co-operation, like feet, like hands, like eyelids, like the rows of the upper and lower teeth. To act against one another then is contrary to nature; and it is acting against one another to be vexed and to turn away.

As Marcus Aurelius advises here, begin from a position in which you assume that you will listen to your teammates, and that anything they do is not going to wound you personally. As a respected team leader, you can find a myriad number of ways to help your teammates have a better working relationship with the coaching staff. By using diplomatic and deferential communication styles, you can function as a liaison between your teammates and the varied personnel in charge of team-related activities. The natural leader can deftly intercede on behalf of individual players. Also, don't be afraid to try humor. When tension reigns in the locker room or practice facility, you should not hesitate to inject some levity into the atmosphere, pulling off tasteful practical jokes and the like.

## Take Care of Your Surroundings

A final word on team leadership and the varied roles you can play for the benefit of those around you—whether you are participating in high school, college, or other sports programs. Take care of your surroundings. Let's imagine, for example, that the grounds surrounding your team's gymnasium, pool, or playing field are defaced with litter. An unimportant point, you say? On the contrary, for when a visiting team gets off the bus, the opposing coach will notice and make appropriate deductions concerning your team's sports program. On an away trip, George Allen, former coach of the Washington Redskins, had just such an experience. When he stepped off the bus, he noticed that the opposing team's stadium parking lot was far from clean. He ordered his players back on the bus and told them something close to the following: "Look out the window. Do you see the litter? Well, the organization here is not taking care of business. We're going to win today." And they did.

Former N.Y. Giants lineman Antonio Pierce is, for the time being, coaching football at Long Beach Polytechnic High, a storied program that has sent fifty-five players over the years to the NFL. Mr. Pierce bemoaned the fact that at the beginning of his tenure at Poly, litter and dinginess marred some of the training facilities. Having cleaned everything up and instituted a regime that cares for the team's surroundings, Mr. Pierce added: "How can you have the morale of a championship program and yet you're in a dungeon? [...] If there's chairs on the floor and trash on the floor, what are they going to do? I told them this is our home for four to five months out of the year; we've got to keep it clean."

As a team leader, it behooves you to make sure that your surroundings are respected. You can go beyond basic cleanliness to create an environment that inspires your teammates, like making several attractive signs with inspirational sayings such as, "When the going gets tough, the tough get going." These signs, with permission from the coach, can be placed strategically inside the locker room.

## KEY TAKEAWAYS

- The respect of coaches and players comes from setting an example and from demonstrating leadership qualities.

- As a team leader, be sensitive and empathetic to the diverse personalities evident among your teammates.

- Take initiatives for the betterment of your teammates, discreetly intervening when one is in trouble or needs medical or psychological attention.

- Take care of your training environment, showing respect by keeping it clean and well-maintained.

# 17

# Being Coachable

*I consider Phil Jackson to be the Dean Smith of the professional game [*
*... ] . He has his own idiosyncrasies and employs psychological warfare*
*to make you think about your mistakes or to understand the team*
*concept. But I respect that. . . . He has to blend egos together so that*
*they have the same team focus.*

—Michael Jordan

**WHEN YOU ARE YOUNG**, you may have, in principle, great athletic potential. However, how you are coached—and how you respond to and take advantage of that coaching—can determine whether that talent will be developed or lie dormant. If you want to succeed as an elite or aspiring athlete, be smart and be coachable. In this chapter, we'll learn two basic strategies for establishing and maintaining a positive relationship with your coach: being a team player and working your hardest at all times. Learn how to study videos to break down an opponent's tendencies. Practice fundamentals over and over and improve on specialized skills and mind-control exercises. Moreover, demonstrate to your coaches and teammates that teamwork is a priority, and that being selfish is not an option.

## Show Your Coach That You Are a Team Player

If you're part of a team sport, creating a good foundation with your coach begins and ends with demonstrating that you will make an important contribution to the team as a whole. Demonstrate that you value being part of the team. Whatever the coach says or does should be interpreted as being in the team's best interest. At the same time, a good coach will invite a player's suggestions or point of view on a troublesome matter. Your opinion should matter to your coach. Know, however, that the coach will always have the last word and it must be honored. If the final decision does not reflect your point of view, accept it with grace.

The coach generally expects teamwork, not diva behavior. For example, if a basketball player is too self-absorbed, he may not look to pass to a free teammate: He is letting the team down and is noticed in a negative light by the coach and scouts. Superiority actually materializes because of hard work and listening to one's coach. Even star players need to put the team first. When the star player is being double and triple-teamed does he or she pass the ball off to the free teammate? Does the football star running-back hustle down the field to make a crucial block? Does the most gifted swimmer pump up her relay swim mates before the sound of the horn?

From the perspective of the coach, the ideal team member, whether humble or boisterous, respects the coach and his teammates. Your self-confidence should never preclude you from carefully listening to the coach and from boosting the morale of your team during difficult moments. Be a coachable individual who arrives on the practice field early and is the last to leave. When other players are injured, you should be there, demonstrating your concern. Essentially, then, become a leader by example. When the coach seeks a frank opinion as to the morale of the team, be the reliable player to whom he or she turns. When a teammate is missing from evening study hall, be the one who gives the absent person a ring or text message.

As concerns such individual sports as golf, tennis, and skiing, athletes may have engaged a personal or professional trainer to elevate their performance to the next level. In these one-on-one situations, athletes must employ mature intelligence and empathy to allow the trainer/coach in question enough extended time to implement their innovative training strategies. Whether the athletes are well known or not should not influence the need for them to remain open-minded and cooperative to the fullest extent when interacting with their coach.

On the professional level (let us take football as an example), the coachable individual can be characterized best by comparing him to his opposite. Without naming names, it is clear that each year a number of teams in the NFL are plagued by one or more individuals who are not satisfied with the play-calling. On the sidelines, the television networks and cable stations zero in on these players' disruptive behavior. Interestingly, bad behavior manifests itself particularly when a team is losing. Fortunately, after several initial years of causing dissension in the ranks, a problematic star player will often begin to take a wiser line of conduct when he realizes that his immediate chances of being hired as a spokesman by Nike or another corporation are nil. Simultaneously, he begins to understand that his chances of eventually becoming a television football analyst are quickly evaporating. The ideal player, then, is one who supports his coaches and teammates, especially in defeat.

And the ideal coach practices these values as well. You may have noticed that some very talented, winning coaches or team leaders often yell at team members, even employing foul language during practice sessions. One could call this type of behavior "motivation through fear." It can be effective; however, it does not take long for word to spread throughout the campus or city that the atmosphere surrounding such-and-such a team is noxious. We have observed that this type of coach changes jobs fairly often, especially in the professional ranks. Moreover, it is our contention that individual leaders who are prone to yelling and temper tantrums are less likely to be able to improvise on the fly when their team is losing.

Show your coach that you will do whatever you can to boost the team's morale. Recently while we were watching a Sunday-night NFL game, one team scored several touchdowns early on. By the second half, this same team was ahead by twenty points. We were shaking our heads in disappointment, but how we felt was nothing compared to the disheartened attitude of the losing team. It truly seemed as if the only animated person on that sideline was the coach who was constantly attempting to motivate his discouraged players. Remember: It does not matter what the scoreboard indicates. Losing or winning, as an elite athlete, you should be performing at your best all of the time. Immediate circumstances can change dramatically in any game or one-on-one competition. Just think back to the 1993 AFC Wild Card playoff game between the Buffalo Bills and the Houston Oilers (now the Tennessee Titans). The score early in the second half was 31 to 3. Well, the Bills came back all the way to an overtime 41–38 victory. Show your coach and your whole team that you never give up! Make it a point of personal pride to play your best both when winning and when losing.

## Go the Extra Mile for Your Coach

The best players distinguish themselves in the eyes of coaches by hard work, day in and day out. During practice, great coaches go over bread-and-butter plays ad infinitum so that excellent execution becomes second nature. The coachable individual understands instinctively the importance of going over and over the basics. Certain athletes may have a hard time accepting a coaching philosophy that gives priority to repeating the fundamentals again and again. The coachable athlete understands how repetition that on the surface appears boring results in reflexive reactions in the heat of competition. For example, as mentioned elsewhere in this book, when coachable basketball team members laboriously and repeatedly drill to counter the full-court press, they are rewarded by being able to instinctively handle any type of press thrown at them in real game situations.

As mentioned above, being coachable means being able to listen to and absorb the coach's words. Taking notes at meetings is part of the process. It also means communicating with coaches if you have an inspired idea that will help the team improve in theory and in actual competition. Interestingly, a player might even speak to coaches about equipment and game-day clothing. For example, you might realize that the game-day football pants lack proper stretch properties or that the face-guard on your hockey helmet partly blocks your vision.

Being coachable, regardless of the sport, means spending a good deal of time studying video and communicating insightful ideas to the appropriate coach or coaches. For example, let us look at a defensive back (named Grayson) on a college team. He has listened to his assistant coach and to scouts who have reported on the basic tendencies of the wide receiver our defensive back will be assigned to. Moreover, Grayson has internalized the coaches' strong suggestion that players take advantage of the media room whose director can provide players with a host of varied, pertinent video footage. As Grayson watches his team's upcoming opponent in action, he comes to realize that the wide receiver he will be covering unintentionally reveals whether he will be a target of a pass or whether he will be just blocking downfield. Grayson has noticed that when the opposing wideout in question breaks the huddle early, he is likely to be the main target of a pass play.

## Coachability for Life

Your efforts at being coachable in sports don't just have dividends in the present. Yes, you will be more likely to earn your coach's respect if you consistently give your best and demonstrate your ability to contribute to a team. But these skills are important for the rest of your life, not just for athletic competition.

Unfortunately, some people never learn the value of teamwork and never learn how to accept constructive criticism appropriately. As they begin their careers outside of sports, they may bring an inflated ego or palpable insecurity with them into the workplace. One study found, for example, that among people who did not succeed at their jobs, the number-one reason for their failure was an inability to be coached by others (26 percent). Coming in at a close second at 23 percent was a lack of "emotional intelligence," which is basically the ability to be sensitive to other people's feelings, responding appropriately in social situations, and being a team player. Rounding out the top four reasons were a lack of motivation and a temperament that was unsuited to the job at hand. In other words, the most significant reasons for adults' job failures were not technical (not having the training or skills to perform assigned tasks) but emotional. They failed at work because they were not coachable.

The good news is that while coachability seems to come more naturally to some people than it does to others, it is a learned trait as much as an inborn characteristic. Writing in *Forbes* magazine, marketing consultant and business leader August Turak speaks of hiring a coach to help him with his golf game and having the coach tell him how refreshing it was to have a client who actually listened to and tried to implement his suggestions. "Augie, I enjoy teaching you," the golf coach told him. "No matter what I ask you to do you give me 150%. You'd be amazed at how many guys pay me just to argue with me. They don't really want to change it; they'd rather be right than good." Upon reflection, August realized that this commitment on his part to being coachable and learning from the best had served him well throughout his life, opening many doors. He identified five traits that individuals can work on to become more coachable:

1. *Humility.* The first step in coachability is realizing that you don't know everything. "Humility teaches that there are things we need to do that we cannot do on our own," he writes.

2. *Action bias.* Essentially, an "action bias" is a commitment to stop merely dreaming. You have to set concrete goals and put them into action, working hard every day to become better.

3. *Purity of purpose.* Turak sees this as a desire to learn for learning's own sake. It's being curious about the world and desiring to make yourself better.

4. *Surrender.* Coachable people are willing to surrender some control so they can learn from experts. This goes hand in hand with humility (#1), because once you have acknowledged that you don't have all the answers you have to be willing to put yourself in a subordinate position to someone who does, at least for a time.

5. *Faith.* Coachable people believe in themselves and their ability to change, even when for a time it seems like the progress is going backwards rather than forwards.

Adopting a coachable attitude will help you not just in sports, but in many other endeavors as well. Consider what it would involve for you to be working on these five traits in the various areas of your life.

## KEY TAKEAWAYS

- Listen carefully to your coaches or professional trainers.
- Use mind control, particularly self-talk, to maintain a positive, focused demeanor when things are not going your way during a competition. Athletes who moan and groan because they do not

like the play-calling or the overall coach-devised strategy are heading quickly towards a no-win situation that may get them into trouble.

- Do not hesitate to take notes during meetings whenever possible and to watch video of upcoming opponents.

- Show your coach through your hard work that you always seek to improve yourself physically, intellectually, and morally.

- Keep in mind that being coachable is a trait you can intentionally cultivate, and that will help you all through your life.

# 18

# Developing Your Mind and Preparing for the Future

*Mens sana in corpore sano.*

—Latin adage meaning "A sound mind in a sound body"

**DAN VALAHU, ONE OF THE AUTHORS**
of this book, was born in Romania, spent five years in Rome, Italy, and then landed up in Elmhurst, Queens (N.Y.C.) at the age of seven. The local boys his age called him "Pinky Roma Pants" for reasons too complicated to elucidate here. As you can imagine, it was very difficult for him to change cultures and especially languages as a child. It was only in graduate school that he, in earnest, began to make a determined effort to improve his diction and pronunciation. He managed it; so can you.

You may be wondering what a chapter on intellectual development is doing in a book that deals with athletic success. After all, isn't it enough just to succeed as an elite athlete? The answer is no. Although your post-sports future may seem very far away, now is the time to commit yourself to preparing your mind for post-athletic professional opportunities. Strong communication skills are a cornerstone of success after your life in sports. For example, you may wish to become a good-will ambassador and spokesperson for a company or a university, and will need to have well-developed communication skills to enable you to give speeches and sound bites to the media. This, in turn, involves reading and listening with care to speakers who have a solid command of the English language. Employers consistently rank communication skills as the single most important qualification they look for in job candidates—even surpassing such things as knowledge and hard work. In many jobs, employees spend around three-quarters of their time communicating with others via meetings, e-mails, phone calls, and memos. What's more, improved communication skills can also help you right now, in sports and in life.

## Work on Your Speaking

Situation: You are already, or desire to be, an elite athlete. You can talk about sports to anyone who is interested and you can give pep talks to your teammates. However, deep inside, you feel intellectually inadequate. Perhaps, in the past, you read newspaper or magazine articles, but never buried your nose inside a book. There are words you hear on a regular basis whose meaning escapes you. When you are with a certain family member-in-law you feel intimidated because he or she speaks fluent, grammatically correct English. You notice that he or she says, "Sylvie and I are going on vacation" whereas you habitually say, "Me and Sylvie are going on vacation." In the above case, after asking a trusted friend, you come to understand that a subject ("I") comes before the verb, not the object form ("me"). Therefore, "Sylvie and I are going on vacation" is correctly spoken.

What to do if you are in this situation and secretly feel insecure about your communication skills? First, no matter what, be yourself, even if you make occasional grammatical errors. If all your time is basically taken up competing or getting ready to compete, just listen to the manner in which coaches and media express themselves, and do not worry about your way of speaking—it is good enough. Others are happy to give you a pass because of your athletic ability. However, if you desire to improve your diction, especially in the off-season, try to attend all your classes. Listen to how your professors and teachers express themselves. Jot down words whose meaning eludes you and look them up in a dictionary. If you wonder about how to pronounce certain words, try an online dictionary that will say the word aloud for you when you press the sound button. Begin to notice the difference between those individuals around you who speak well and those who do not. Do not be afraid to change the manner in which you pronounce words and sentences.

An excellent way to improve your speaking skills is to record yourself reading out loud on your phone or mobile device, and then listen to the playback. In this way, you get the benefit of practice from reading aloud and can hear how you sound to other people. Moreover, there exist terrific podcasts and news apps you can listen to. For example, downloading the NPR app and choosing four or five stories (or interviews) a day to listen to would help you improve communication skills and knowledge of the world we live in. Many great speakers throughout history, including Demosthenes (c. 384–322 B.C.) turned to various types of vocal practice to improve the pronunciation, clarity, and power of their voice.

A last point in the above context: When you are given any opportunity to talk to an audience, whether at a high school assembly or a professional gathering, say yes. True, you may feel nervous about public speaking. Don't worry, you will do fine. Those individuals who are intimidated by this can join an evening Dale Carnegie Course on public speaking or a local chapter of Toastmasters International. Whether or not you take such a course, remember that statistical studies have shown that 90 percent of speakers experience at least some anxiety before delivering a speech. In fact, Gallup has found that public speaking is the second-most-common fear among American adults (the first is snakes). It should comfort you to know that if you don't automatically enjoy speaking in public, you're not alone. However, with practice you can build your skill in this area so that you are no longer afraid and even begin to enjoy public speaking.

## Expand Your Reading

If strong communication skills are vital for your success in life after sports, then their foundation is laid by regular reading. Reading is a core skill that's fundamental for doing well at other things, yet a growing number of people read little or not at all. According to the National Institute for Literacy, 20 percent of U.S. adults read on a fifth-grade level or lower, which makes them basically ineligible for jobs with higher salaries. Athletes are often affected by this trend. At the University of North Carolina, one study showed that more than half of the school's athletes read below an eighth-grade level—and these were athletes who had been accepted to college.

Remember that reading is a learned skill, not a natural trait. Just like any skill you've learned as an athlete, you can improve your fluency and comprehension with added practice. To develop this ability, start by reading more than sports websites or the sports page in the daily newspaper. Look for interesting non-sports stories you can relate to on such news sites as nytimes.com or usatoday.com. In your field of prowess, be it basketball, football, track, tennis, and so on, buy or consult magazines that specialize in your sport at bookstores and libraries. If you are not sure what to read, begin with *Sports Illustrated*. It is a well-written weekly magazine that has interesting sports-related articles and a strong online presence at si.com. Following this initiative, graduate to consuming several print magazines a week, or challenging yourself to read a certain number of articles each week online.

So, now you are listening carefully to how others express themselves; you are reading newspapers and magazines. If what we have suggested up to this point does not resonate with you and you do not care to preoccupy yourself with this type of intellectual development, do not worry; just go on being yourself, concentrating fully on the sport you love and in which you excel. If, however, what has been suggested above appeals to you, continue reading. Once you are seeing the benefits of reading the newspaper and specialized magazines, it is time to graduate to the next level. One of the best introductions to reading books is Louis L'Amour's *Education of a Wandering Man*. In an easy-to-read manner, L'Amour chronicles his early experience with book reading. For people interested in improving the way they speak and becoming more conversant with and knowledgeable about the world's best literature, this book is a must. L'Amour takes the reader on his personal journey through some of the most interesting must-reads in the world of literature.

After reading Louis L'Amour's *Education of a Wandering Man*, switch to Mortimer Adler's classic *How to Read a Book*. Then, enjoy and instruct yourself with two vocabulary-oriented books by Norman Lewis: *30 Days to a More Powerful Vocabulary* and *Word Power Made Easy*. Read them in the above order. At this point, assuming you have finished the above-mentioned books, you are on your way. From this point on, be careful to choose books to read which you are sure will interest you, perhaps biographies of heroes in your sport. While on the bus or airplane, or during your spare time, embark on the habit of reading. Let others listen to music or sleep; you are interested in elevating your intellectual and cultural horizons. Again, of course, if none of the above interests you, forget about it. Continue to be who you are, and strive to be the best athlete you can be. The language and intellectual education referred to above will come to you one way or another as you mature.

## Prepare for a Life After Sports

From the start of your sports career to its end, as an elite athlete you should occasionally reflect on the future. In social and financial terms, you must prepare for life after the game. The majority of high school and college athletes will not have careers in professional sports, so even if turning pro is your dream be sure to have an alternate career plan you are preparing for. If you are fortunate enough to be among the relatively small group of athletes who become paid professionals, be aware it will not last forever. You should expect to retire from sports at some point, either from age or injury. Too many athletes stay around longer than necessary for predictable reasons: they have not invested money wisely or put enough aside; they miss being in the limelight; or they love the game and the camaraderie too much to leave.

Think in advance about the career you may want to pursue after you graduate from college or retire from professional sports. Choose a profession and study up on it. If you intend to become a television sports analyst, for example, it is never too early to improve on your speaking ability, grammar, and voice projection. Prepare like you did when training as an athlete. For example, hire private tutors if you can afford to do so; then, when it is time, you are not going in blind. Work on your intellect: read, listen, write letters, take notes, or keep a diary. You can engage a wise family counselor or life coach to learn how to familiarize yourself with these initiatives. If you lack experience in the intricacies of a chosen field, do not try to do everything by yourself. As mentioned above, you may be in a position to hire private experts in the particular field that is of interest to you. If that's not feasible, there exist free online resources such as mappingyourfuture. org and bridgestowork.org that will help tutor you in your chosen field.

Some well-known athletes may decide to enter upon a post-professional career having nothing to do with sports or public speaking. For example, quite a few professional football, baseball, and hockey players have opened up restaurants. Others, like Mark Spitz, have become successful real estate agents. Nonetheless, these individuals do speak with clients. The fluency of their English, while not a determining factor, does make an impression.

Getting ready for a career can provide pleasure. If you are an elite athlete, you already know how to meet any challenge you have decided to take on. These same skills will be invaluable in your work life. Be a champion at anything you set your mind to. Keep your body and mind fit; still set goals and prepare for success. A fine example of what we are suggesting is embodied in the multiple ambitions of Yannick Agnel, the 6' 8" French swimming phenomenon we met in an earlier chapter. Agnel was the 2012 Olympic and 2014 world champion in the 200-meter freestyle. More to the point, Agnel is taking correspondence courses in economics and political science. Despite the intense workouts designed by his coach, he is committed to continuing his education.

Before closing this chapter, a word on financial planning for the athlete. At the beginning of a professional career you need to find a dedicated, trustworthy financial advisor who will invest money wisely. Find a "fee-only" financial counselor whose salary is not based on commissions from selling you various financial products. You can find such a professional in your area by searching the website of the National Association of Personal Finance Advisors (www.napfa.org); just type in your zip code and the organization will provide you with a list of professionals where you live. If you are not sure in whom to place your trust, give McCormick's International Management Group your blessing. Before choosing a financial advisor or company, consider buying the CD program *Understanding Investments* taught by economics professor Connel Fullenkamp of Duke University (http://www.thegreatcourses.com/courses/understanding-investments.html).

Structure the account(s) in such a way that the adviser has no access to assets; that is, the account must be in your name only. Moreover, never live a lifestyle that eats up both salary and savings. This is not an easy thing to do when all around you teammates and other friends are buying large homes and expensive cars. Diversify investments. Read books on finance; educate yourself so you understand what your trusted investor is telling you. If reading about personal financial security is not your thing, then take a personal finance course. Such courses exist for people who are about to enter the professional ranks. Another possibility: set up a series of meetings with a well-regarded professor of finance management or the like. It is your money, so it is important to take time out to learn where it is going and why. Being able to live well during retirement on the interest of previously well-invested funds is crucial. Do not worry about keeping up with what everyone else is doing with their money; focus on safe investments or savings strategies.

A few last tips to invest your money wisely:

- Do not trust strangers or so-called "friends" offering you strange deals. Watch out for slick con artists.
- Always be in complete control of your assets.
- Do not make hasty financial decisions.
- Keep a close eye on your investments.

## KEY TAKEAWAYS

- Communication skills are vital to your success in life after sports, and are ranked by employers as the most important qualification they're seeking when people apply for a job.

- Build your communication skills by reading widely, speaking in public whenever you have the opportunity, and expanding your vocabulary. There is great value in simply reading texts out loud.

- Save your money. When it comes time for investing a portion of it, make absolutely certain that your financial advisor is a "fee-only" professional.

- Most people who have success as elite athletes when they are young will not become professional athletes, so it's important to prepare yourself for a career you will enjoy.

# 19

# Coaching for Victory, Coaching for Life

*But as a coach, the key to building bonds between players and you is being truly invested in them. [...] Spending time with them and understanding what is important to them is critical.*

—Art Briles

## ONE DAY YOU MAY WANT TO

become a coach. The best way to become a great one is to have the respect of your players and coaching staff. As you imagine your future after elite sports, coaching can be a natural outgrowth of all you have learned and a way of giving back to others. In this chapter, we'll highlight some of the characteristics of top coaches— which, you will not be surprised to learn, are similar to the characteristics of top athletes we have already covered. Great coaches have high expectations and achievable goals, just like great athletes. They are consistent and fair with their athletes, not playing favorites or throwing temper tantrums. They work hard to earn respect and maintain healthy relationships with the people around them.

## Have High Expectations

Legendary football coach Vince Lombardi was not always liked and his practices were anything but fun. In fact, when he led the Green Bay Packers, workouts were often brutal. Plays were drilled endlessly until even the nuances of the playbook were executed flawlessly. Lombardi was a teacher with very high expectations of his athletes. He not only went over every possible aspect of a play or defensive scheme, but he explained in exhaustive detail why each was important. For example, he took great pains to demonstrate the lineman's stance. Lombardi would begin early-season practice by showing a seasoned lineman the proper form of the basic three-point stance. This was no joke. The essence of the lesson was to position the body in such a way that (1) the opposition could not tell whether the play was a run or a pass and (2) the lineman could explode forward and laterally as well as sure-footedly move backwards to protect on pass plays. As a coach, Lombardi did not let any detail escape his notice.

Lombardi's insistence on exhaustively practicing offensive plays and defensive schemes from the playbook is no different from reading and re-reading successive drafts of an essay or a paper you have written. When I (Dan Valahu) worked for the Hospital Corporation of America (HCA), my specialty was to create multiple-choice SAT-type questions for nurses. These questions were designed to test the level of empathy of each nurse who took the test. When I finished the first version of the questionnaire, my boss told me to take the test myself. I was puzzled since I had taken great pains to get it right. Well, when I took it, I was amazed at how many mistakes and ambiguities I found. So, Lombardi was correct in insisting that his team "rehearse" in depth any and all plays that might be called during a game. Lombardi wisely took the adage that "practice makes perfect" literally.

Lombardi saw himself as an emotional, fiery leader who did not brook laziness or insubordination. At the same time, he harbored a generous spirit: upon arriving at Green Bay, he invited players, spouses, staff, and anyone else working at the football complex to a cookout he hosted. Many were immediately won over by Coach Lombardi's manner of speaking, the content of his words, his posture, and general demeanor, and they became converts to his stringent system. At its core, the system demanded that players come to practice fully prepared mentally and that they be daily committed to an all-out physical effort. His twice-daily practices lasted only one and one-half hours each, but they were intense and highly organized. If a player did not totally buy into the system, he was gone. Though Lombardi was tough on his players, he was far from being a martinet: Willie Wood called him "perhaps the fairest person I ever met."

Changing the existing culture at Green Bay was not effected overnight. Following several two-a-day practices, Lombardi was reduced to a state of severe disappointment. The ineptitude he witnessed had permeated most of the team. Lombardi was determined to change that culture. One morning he walked into the training room full of Green Bay players receiving treatment for one sort of ailment or another. He is quoted as having admonished the sorry group for paying too much attention to minor aches and pains. He made it clear that he never wanted to witness such a spectacle again. In his first talk to the fully-assembled team he instituted an eleven o'clock curfew (midnight on Saturday) and made it clear that lateness to meetings or visits to bars would elicit hefty fines.

Lombardi demanded that his players possess a relentlessly imperturbable, invincible attitude on the field of battle. Not only did Lombardi expect perfection of execution on the field, but he was adamant that his players be dressed in blazers and ties whenever the team travelled. Moreover, Lombardi was ultra-strict about punctuality: "on time" to him meant arriving five or ten minutes early. Coach Lombardi's football philosophy and its implementation by his players soon led to victory in the first two Super Bowls (1967 and 1968).

While Lombardi's aggressive nature may not be for everyone, anyone who aspires to become a coach can benefit from his dedication to excellence. He used his voice and strong body language to mark his players from the very first day of his coaching tenure. He came across as a highly organized individual who confidently believed in what he was doing. Whenever he spoke to individuals or to the team as a whole, Lombardi communicated in a clear, articulate manner. At the same time, it became obvious early on that he expected everyone to buy into his system. At the very first team meeting, he made it understood that practicing the fundamentals of football was crucial to ensuring success on the field. Repetition would become the supreme value. Lombardi made things simple; what had been complicated in the past (signal calling and blocking assignments, for example) became simplified and thus more easily memorized and executed.

Lombardi demanded hard work from his players on the practice field and a focused intellectual mastery of the playbook. In exchange, he promised his team that he would be relentless in his effort to make each player the best he could be.

This meant sacrifice and the spurning of instant gratification by both players and coaches. Individual pursuit of glory needed to be sublimated for the common good.

Great coaches insist on the very best from their players and structure every practice to further the pursuit of excellence. Repetition until an action becomes a reflex can be applied to any sport. Take basketball, for instance. Why is it that a full-court press often rattles an opposing team? The reason is that their coach has not drilled the recognition of myriad defensive formations and the responses to them. Great coaching means that the team has worked tirelessly on every aspect of the game to the point that regardless of the situation on the court, the team seamlessly shifts into the proper and effective antidote, neutralizing whatever is thrown at them.

Great coaches come prepared, having educated themselves on the competition. Scouting the "other" team is an art form. If the scouting team is effective, then the coach can construct valuable training sessions that fully prepare a team to recognize and properly react to the other team's on-the-court strategies. In this context, it would seem valuable to assign a video expert to create a series of videos, repeatedly highlighting the most common penalty-producing mistakes, both offensively and defensively. For example, take the kickoff in football. The videos would show numerous examples of every common error made by the kicking team as well as the receiving unit. Players involved would be obliged to watch the videos repeatedly, until they could recite a basic litany of commonplace errors to the coach.

## Be Consistent and Fair

Although his coaching made him a household name, John Wooden was not interested in personal fame. He was invested in getting the most out of each of his players by treating them as individuals and not as recruited athletes who would be gone in a few years to be replaced by other players. This equal-opportunity approach characterizes all great coaches, who meticulously go over the fundamentals with each player regardless of who is considered a "star." Coach Wooden's four P's were planning, preparation, practice, and performance. In team sports, the best coaches are focused on the big picture of what will work for the whole team, regardless of the varying talents and contributions of the individual players. In turn, the players of these coaches desire to win as a fully-integrated unit, intent on teamwork.

Wooden took the UCLA basketball team to unheard-of heights in the 1960s and 70s, winning ten out of twelve NCAA championships (including seven in a row). He was extremely demanding, but he was fair. His workouts were short and intense. Players were exhausted at the end of practice, but they understood that they would be in better shape than their opponents. Wooden's idea of conditioning was related not only to the physical aspects of the game, but also to a moral and mental conditioning. He worked hard to promote a strong work ethic, character, and citizenship. As a player, you were in trouble if you cut a class, fell behind, did not attend evening study hall, or were not ambitious about knowledge and good grades. On the court, the individual gave way to teamwork and the open-player philosophy. Interestingly, his players, though thoroughly schooled in the basics and able to execute plays reflexively, were trained to remain alert and observant in order to be able to improvise whenever the situation called for it. In the final analysis his teams were always poised and confident, regardless of the immediate score. They evinced self-control, alertness, and initiative. Above all, the individual player redirected his own prowess in favor of the team's interest.

## Invest in Personal Relationships

Coach Wooden wasn't just renowned for his winning strategies on the court and the fairness with which he treated each player. He was also famous for the close personal relationships he cultivated with them. While many college coaches are closer to their players during their undergraduate playing days than they are after graduation, with coach Wooden the reverse was true. He kept in close touch with his departed players, answering their letters with his own hand-written missives, while helping them to become model citizens. The best coaches recognize that being a mentor isn't just something that happens when you're doing sports; it extends to all aspects of life. Through it all Wooden made sure never to play favorites. The players were his sons, each the equal of any other son.

The counter-culture of the 1960s and 1970s had no influence whatsoever on coach Wooden. Take, for example, his relationship with Bill Walton, who played center on the UCLA teams of the early 1970s. Walton was a free spirit who in many ways looked like and behaved like the hippies of that era. However, while he was in coach Wooden's presence, on and off the court, Walton adhered to Wooden's rules. If Walton's hairstyle did not meet with Wooden's directives, Walton was "excused" from practice until he corrected the problem. Today, Walton is in his mid-sixties. He now attributes his success in life to the sacrifice, discipline, and sound moral code he absorbed, sometimes against his will, during the four years he played for Coach Wooden.

Successful coaches are able to control their emotions, particularly fear, anger, and other debilitating feelings. For example, let us imagine a soccer semifinal match during which a referee erroneously draws a red card on team A, which goes on to lose in the last minutes. Following the final whistle, the coach of team A could run after the guilty referee and berate him in front of the fans; or, she could remain calm, dignified, and aware that there are official mechanisms in place for scolding the referee in question. In the meantime, the coach of team A quickly congratulates team B's players and coaches and heads to the locker room where she consoles her forces with one of the most eloquent and moving speeches of her career. Team A players are primed to win the consolation match and to reassemble next year to follow the path that leads to hoisting the division trophy.

To be a great leader you have to know how to listen to and understand your players. You need to remain open-minded because every player is different. You may be able to confront some players in the presence of others, while other players need to be taken aside lest they shut down with regard to communication. Whatever your style, your players must willingly buy into your system. Some coaches are introverts, while others are expansive. Phil Jackson, the former coach of the Chicago Bulls basketball team, was a master at convincing some of his top scorers to be model players. He could get the best out of all his players because he knew what made each of them tick, what would set them off, or what would motivate them. He developed personal relationships with each member of his squad. Consequently, each player believed that he truly cared about them. Having this type of relationship with players will make them go above and beyond what is expected of them.

Remarkable coaches understand their players' preferred learning style. For example, swim coach Kim Brackin says that athletes of the Millennial generation "prefer to hear stories that document what they are learning. They want to be involved in the conversation and to give their opinion. They want to see images that help them process. And lastly, they appreciate when you can keep concepts simple." Coach Brackin goes on to highlight the importance of showing athletes of this visually-minded generation actual footage of themselves in action. The reaction of the viewing athlete is often one of disbelief, a disbelief that translates into deep learning and improvement. She advises coaches to accumulate a library of footage depicting athletes performing their skill optimally. Individuals or a group of athletes can then view and re-view this footage at their leisure.

Many players attribute their success in life to the values and principles that their coaches exemplified. The coaches we are speaking of were interested in the player's family life, studies, and after-sports career. Kansas State's football coach, Bill Snyder, writes handwritten notes to his players after games, offering encouragement or expressing "his admiration regardless of the outcome." Interestingly, Snyder pens letters to opposing players as well. After a game with Texas Tech, Snyder wrote to Jace Amaro: "You've had a great year, Jace. Admire how hard you play and the innate toughness you display to help your team. Hope you weren't hurt badly on Saturday. Wishing you and your teammates continued success, good fortune and health." Overall, Snyder writes hundreds of letters each season to fellow coaches as well as players and recruits.

As a coach, it's also vital that you develop strong relationships with your assistant coaches. Surround yourself with a good coaching staff. Share responsibility and let them teach what they know best. Be willing to get feedback, even if it is critical of your methods, and let them do things that you are not familiar with. Delegating tasks will lower stress so you, the head coach, can concentrate more on the big picture. Henry Ford couldn't build a car, but he was smart enough to hire individuals who could!

To get to know his players better, Jim Caldwell, head coach of the Detroit Lions, lets them choose a restaurant where they would like to dine. There he asks them about their backgrounds, interests, and families, and tells stories about his career, the people who have influenced him the most, and his children and grandchildren. For some of the Detroit players it is the first time that a coach has invited them to dinner, or spoken so candidly about his personal life. This gives Caldwell some moral authority for giving advice to the players, such as when he told them that instead of focusing on their reputation as bad boys, they would earn the respect they yearned for "by playing in a respectful way."

In sum, we can say that the greatest coaches are intent on teaching about life. They care about the growth of their players as human beings.

## KEY TAKEAWAYS

- Outstanding coaches work with team leaders to defuse the onset of discouragement and dissatisfaction.
- Great coaches find effective ways to motivate each of their players, and develop personal relationships with them.
- Effective coaches are not fearful of constantly going back to the basics. Repetition is the key.
- Being demanding but fair appears to be a basic tenet of good coaching.

# Appendix A

# Master Hill's Philosophical Pointers

1. Be gracious and even-tempered in victory and defeat; come back strong from defeat or injury.
2. Maintain a perpetual state of improvement physically, mentally, and morally.
3. Remember: each one of us is part of the same human family.
4. Literally, you are what you eat.
5. Try not to overestimate or underestimate your teammates and the people you meet. Be patient. Get to know them.
6. Relentlessly perfect the basics in your sports field.
7. Praise and create happiness for others.
8. Honesty, though sometimes painful, is the best option.
9. Accept responsibility for your actions or non-actions.
10. Remain open to the advice and criticism of others.
11. If you make a mistake, be vigilant not to repeat it. Apologize, if appropriate.
12. Be ready both physically and mentally for each contest.
13. Choose a financial adviser or organization with extreme care.
14. Beyond power, strength, speed, agility, and endurance, do not forget flexibility and reflex work.
15. Carpe Diem: Seize the day!
16. Treat individuals as you yourself would like to be treated.
17. Self-discipline, tenacity, and imperturbability are the best formulas to ensure the attainment of your goals.
18. When you say, "How are you?" be sincere.
19. Reflect on the joy of living.
20. Never give up working to fulfill your dreams.

## Motivational quotes from Master Hill:

❖ "Fear can be overcome by the desire to be great."

❖ "To get a knockout you must be willing to take a few hits."

❖ "There's never been a victory achieved without blood, sweat, and pain; so suck it up, and stay on the task ahead."

❖ "Champions don't have time to wipe off the blood and dirt; they keep pushing until victory is achieved."

❖ "Don't cry in defeat; don't waste your energy; save it for victory."

# Appendix B

# Two Motivational Texts

Out of the night that covers me,
Black as the Pit from pole to pole,
I thank whatever gods may be
For my unconquerable soul.

In the fell clutch of circumstance
I have not winced nor cried aloud.
Under the bludgeonings of chance
My head is bloody, but unbowed.

Beyond this place of wrath and tears
Looms but the horror of the shade,
And yet the menace of the years
Finds, and shall find me, unafraid.

It matters not how strait the gate,
How charged with punishments the scroll,
I am the master of my fate:
I am the captain of my soul.

—William Ernest Henley, *Invictus*

There is a tide in the affairs of men,
Which, taken at the flood, leads on to fortune;
Omitted, all the voyage of their life
Is bound in shallows and in miseries.
On such a full sea are we now afloat;
And we must take the current when it serves,
Or lose our ventures.

—William Shakespeare, *Julius Caesar*

# Appendix C
# Quotes from Admired World Athletes and Coaches

❖ "Impossible is just a big word thrown around by small men who find it easier to live in the world they've been given than to explore the power they have to change it. Impossible is not a fact, it's an opinion. Impossible is not a declaration, it's a dare. Impossible is potential. Impossible is temporary. Impossible is nothing." – *Muhammad Ali, world heavyweight champion*

❖ "If you are afraid of failure you don't deserve to be successful!" – *Charles Barkley, NBA star and Olympic gold medalist in basketball*

❖ "It's not whether you get knocked down; it's whether you get up." – *Vince Lombardi, professional football coach*

❖ "Today I will do what others won't do so tomorrow I can accomplish what others can't." – *Jerry Rice, football player*

❖ "Talent is God-given. Be humble. Fame is man-given. Be grateful. Conceit is self-given. Be careful." – *John Wooden, college basketball coach*

❖ "What do you do with a mistake: recognize it, admit it, learn from it, forget it." – *Dean Smith, college basketball coach*

❖ "Somewhere behind the athlete you've become and the hours of practice and the coaches who have pushed you is a little girl who fell in love with the game and never looked back . . . play for her." – *Mia Hamm, Olympic gold-medal winner in soccer*

❖ "You can't get much done in life if you only work on the days when you feel good." – *Jerry West, basketball player*

❖ "I've got a theory that if you give 100 percent all of the time, somehow things will work out in the end." – *Larry Bird, basketball player*

❖ "If you play your heart out for what your jersey says on the front, everyone will remember what the jersey says on the back." – *Miracle (film about the 1980 U.S. Men's hockey team)*

❖ "It's hard to beat a person who never gives up." – *Babe Ruth, baseball player*

❖ "Procrastination is one of the most common and deadliest of diseases and its toll on success and happiness is heavy." – *Wayne Gretzky, hockey player*

❖ "I play to win, whether during practice or a real game. And I will not let anything get in the way of me and my competitive enthusiasm to win." – *Michael Jordan, basketball player*

❖ "Let your workings remain a mystery. Just show people the results." – *Lao Tzu, philosopher*

❖ "If you always put limits on everything you do, physical or anything else, it will spread into your work and into your life. There are only plateaus, and you must not stay there, you must go beyond them." – *Bruce Lee, martial artist*

❖ "Pain is temporary. It may last a minute, or an hour, or a day, or a year, but eventually it will subside and something else will take its place. If I quit, however, it lasts forever." – *Lance Armstrong, cyclist*

❖ "You can't make a great play unless you do it first in practice." – *Chuck Noll, football coach*

❖ "Most people get excited about games, but I've got to be excited about practice, because that's my classroom." – *Pat Summitt, basketball coach*

❖ "Leadership is more about responsibility than ability." – *Jim Tunney, NFL referee*

❖ "To be as good as it can be a team has to buy into what you as the coach are doing. They have to feel you're a part of them and they're a part of you." – *Bobby Knight, basketball coach*

❖ "Never quit. It is the easiest cop-out in the world. Set a goal and don't quit until you attain it. When you do attain it, set another goal, and don't quit until you reach it. Never quit." – *Bear Bryant, football coach*

❖ "A winner never whines." – *Paul Brown, football coach*

❖ "Good teams become great ones when the members trust each other enough to surrender the 'me' for the 'we.'" – *Phil Jackson, basketball coach*

❖ "Champions keep playing until they get it right." – *Billie Jean King, tennis champion*

❖ "It is not the strongest of the species that survives, nor the most intelligent, but the one most responsive to change." – *Charles Darwin, scientist*

# For Further Reading

Adler, Alfred. *Understanding Human Nature* (1969).

Alfremow, Jim. *The Champion's Mind: How Great Athletes Think, Train, and Thrive* (2013).

Anderson, Bob. *Stretching* (2000).

Anderson, Owen. *Running Science* (2014).

Broad, William J. *The Science of Yoga: The Risks and the Rewards* (2004).

Butler, Gillian and Tony Hope. *Managing Your Mind* (2007).

Cabane, Olivia Fox. *The Charisma Myth: How Anyone Can Master the Art and Science of Personal Magnetism* (2012).

Cerutty, Percy. *Running with Cerutty* (*Track and Field News*, 1959).

Chapman, Mike. *Legends of the Mat* (2006).

Chapman, Mike. *Wrestling Tough* (2005).

Chichester, Brian and Jack Croft. *Powerfully Fit: Dozens of Ways to Boost Strength, Increase Endurance and Chisel your Body*. Men's Health Series (1996).

Chu, Donald and Gregory Myer. *Plyometrics: Dynamic Strength and Explosive Power* (2013).

Collins, Paul. *Kettlebell Conditioning: Functional Strength, Powerbells* (2011).

Coué, Emile. *Self Mastery Through Conscious Autosuggestion* (1957).

Darden, Ellington. *The New High Intensity Training* (2004).

Fast, Julius. *Body Language* (2002).

Finn, Adharanand. *Running with the Kenyans: Discovering the Secrets of the Fastest People of Earth* (2013).

Grover, Tim. *Relentless: From Good to Unstoppable* (2013).

Hannan, Paul and John Selby. *Take Charge of your Mind* (2006).

Horrowitz, Jeff. *Quick Strength for Runners* (2013).

Jagot, Horice Lance. *Core: The Trainer's Inside Guide to Your Workout* (2013).

Jamison, Steve and John Wooden. *Wooden on Leadership* (2005).

Jagot, Paul. *Méthode Pratique d'Autosuggestion.* (1972).

Kadans, Joseph. *The Encyclopedia of Fruits, Vegetables, Nuts and Seeds For Healthy Living* (2013).

Kurz, Thomas. *Science of Sports Training: How to Control Training for Peak Performance*. Second edition (2001).

Liebman, Horice Lance. *Core: The Trainers Inside Guide to Your Workout* (2013).

Liebman, Joshua. *Peace of Mind* (1966).

Livingston, Keith. *Healthy Intelligent Training: The Proven Principles of Arthur Lydiard* (2009).

Loehr, James, Ed.D. *The New Toughness Training for Sports* (1995).

Lopez, Mario with Jeff O'Connell. *Knockout Fitness* (2008).

Mack, Gary. *Mind Gym: An Athlete's Guide to Inner Excellence* (2001).

Mackenzie, Brian, with Glen Cordoza. *Power Speed Endurance* (2012)

Maltz, Maxwell. *Five Minutes to Happiness* (1967).

Maltz, Maxwell. *Psycho-Cybernetics* (1967).

Maraniss, David. *When Pride Still Mattered: A Life of Vince Lombardi* (1999).

McCloskey, John and Julian Bailes. *When Winning Costs Too Much: Steroids, Supplements and Scandal in Today's Sports* (2006).

Medina, John. *Brain Rules: 12 Principles for Surviving and Thriving at Work, Home, and School* (2008).

Mignault, Lorraine. *Die Healthy* (2004).

Orton, Eric. *The Cool Impossible* (2014).

Paoli, Carl and Anthony Sherbondy. *Freestyle: Maximize Sport and Life Performance with Four Basic Movements* (2014).

Radcliffe, James and Robert Farentinos. *High-Powered Plyometrics* (1999).

Rath, Matthias, M.D. *Why People Get Heart Attacks* (2011).

Roizen, Michael and Mehmet Oz. *YOU: The Owner's Manual: An Insider's Guide to the Body That Will Make You Healthy and Young* (2012).

Rooney, Martin. *Warrior Cardio: The Revolutionary Metabolic Training System for Burning Fat, Building Muscle, and Getting Fit* (2010).

Rubin, Theodore Isaac. *The Winner's Notebook* (1972).

Satchidana, Moliak, Yogiraj. *Integral Yoga Hatha* (1970).

Schuler, Lou and Alwyn Cosgrove. *The New Rules of Lifting For Life: All New Muscle Building, Fat Blasting, Plan for Men and Women Who Want to Ace Their Midlife Exams* (2012).

Sears, Barry. *Enter the Zone* (1995).

Sheridan, Sam. *The Fighter's Mind: Inside the Mental Game* (2010).

Stoop, David. *You Are What You Think* (2003).

Straka, Mike. *Rowdy Rousey: Ronda Rousey's Fight to the Top* (2015).

Suchard, Lior. *Mind Reader* (2012).

Sweeney, Michael. *Brain: The Complete Mind: How It Develops, How It Works, and How to Keep It Sharp* (2014).

Tracy, Brian. *No Excuses: The Power of Self-Discipline* (2010).

Viscott, David. *How to Live with Another Person* (1974).

Wiseman, Richard. *59 Seconds: Change Your Life in Under a Minute* (2003).

Yessis, Michael. *Explosive Running: Using the Science of Kinesiology to Improve Your Performance* (2000).

# About the Authors

Born and raised in Louisiana, **DAVID HILL** now lives in Hewitt, Texas with his wife Laura and their daughter Lauren. David and Laura also have three grown children and three grandchildren. David has an 8th degree black belt. He was International Kickboxing Champion (WKA) for six straight years (1986–1993) with a record of fifty-four victories and four defeats. David was inducted into the Martial Arts Hall of Fame in 2003. He has a personal business in fitness, boxing, martial arts, and is an inspirational speaker. He is also the author of *A Journey in Faith: Parenthood 101*. David has contributed to this volume from the perspective of his personal experience of training for and winning three World Titles in kickboxing (WKA). He is a U.S.A. certified Boxing Coach and Ground Grappling Instructor, as well as a Master Instructor in Tae Kwon Do and Hopkido.

**DAN VALAHU** was an all N.Y. City and State football halfback in high school, and played football and swam in college. He coached high school basketball before and after receiving his Ph.D. in French Language and Literature from Columbia University. In 1994 he completed the Kona, Hawaii Gatorade Ironman Triathlon in thirteen hours. He is now retired from teaching at Baylor University in Waco, Texas and coaches individuals in track and swimming.

# Acknowledgements

Sincerely, we thank our family and friends for their support, prayers, and patience, and for giving us the opportunity to pursue our dreams. A special thanks to Esmeralda Sawyer and Mireille Fantini for their typing and editing of the first manuscript drafts. Appreciation goes out to David M. Uber who read an early version of the manuscript, making corrections and a number of insightful suggestions related to the overall organization of the manuscript.

The authors wish to thank Shelly Taylor for her professional camera work. She is responsible for the excellent photos found in the book. We recognize, with gratitude, Robbie Little, who gave us access to the WRS Fitness Club to photograph athletes Laura Brown and Victor Johnson in motion. Chris Goss not only participated in the photo shoot but was the sole participant in the original photo spread. We are grateful to the designers at Paraclete Press for their work on the cover and the interior layout. Finally, we extend our sincere thanks to Kyle Williams who made a special trip to WRS to provide us with the necessary equipment for the final photo shoot.

# Notes

## Chapter 1: Controlling Your Mind and Emotions

The story about the Villanova-Seton Hall game appeared in a 16 February 2015 Associated Press article ("Barrum Hilliard II helps No. 6 Nova crush Seton Hall"). John Danaher is quoted in Sam Sheridan's *The Fighter's Mind: Inside the Mental Game* (New York: Grove Press, 2010), 237. The story about Michael Jordan is recounted in Tim S. Grover, *Relentless: From Good to Great to Unstoppable* (co-written with Shari Lesser Wenk). See http://20secondtimeout.blogspot.com/2013/04/time-grovers-re. This book delivers the message that physical prowess can only take you so far; it is mental dominance which makes you unstoppable.

Gillian Butler and Tony Hope's interesting book *Managing Your Mind: The Mental Fitness Guide* (Oxford: Oxford University Press, 1995) offers strategies for identifying and managing your emotions. David Stoop addresses the distinction between positive and negative self-talk in *You are What you Think* (Grand Rapids: Revell, 2003), 106–108.

Auto-suggestion is introduced in Paul C. Jagot, *Méthode Pratique d'Autosuggestion* (Paris: Editions Dangles, 1972), 68. Translation by Dan Valahu. The steps of auto-suggestion are adapted and expanded from Emile Coué, *Self Mastery Through Conscious Autosuggestion* (London: George Allen & Unwin Ltd, 1967), 15–16.

## Chapter 2: Visualization

Olympian Dana Hee's story is found in Jim Afremow, *In the Champion's Mind: How Great Athletes Think, Train, and Thrive* (New York: Rodale, 2013), 195.

Maxwell Maltz, *Psycho-Cybernetics* (New York: Essandess Special Edition, 1967), xi. Maltz is also the author of *Five Minutes to Happiness: How to Achieve*

*Happiness*, which is the source of the quote about tricking our nervous system (New York: Grosset & Dunlap, 1962), 50.

The story of East African runners' quest for the sub-two-hour marathon is discussed by Alex Hutchinson, "What Will It Take to Run a 2-Hour Marathon?" in *Runner's World* magazine (November 2014), 78, accessible online at http://rw.runnersworld.com/sub-2/.

According to Arnold Schwarzenegger, as related in the article "Mind over Matter," (*Muscle Magazine* 139 [March 2007], www.emusclemag.com), the biggest muscle of all is the mind. In fact, if individual athletes hope to develop their body, they must control the mind. See pages 141–44.

Michael Sweeney tells about the visualization techniques of Jack Niklaus in his comprehensive and interesting book, *Brain: The Complete Mind* (Washington D.C.: National Geographic, 2009), 156. *Mind Gym: An Athlete's Guide to Inner Excellence* (New York: McGraw-Hill, 2001), 15–16, is Gary Mack's hymn to hard work, fearlessness, and visualization on the way to elite sport stardom.

See also Mario Lopez, *Knockout Fitness: The Six-Week Plan for Sculpting Your Best Body Ever* (New York: Rodale, 2008), 94.

# Chapter 3: The Outside World Does Not Control Our Thoughts

In *Take Charge of Your Mind*, (Newburyport: Hampton Roads Publishing, 2006), Paul Hannam and John Selby define mind-control strategies as "mind-management tools." Early in their volume, they state: "Just as in physical fitness, everyone can actively enhance their mental powers and improve their performance results by learning . . . mind-management tools" (14).

# Chapter 4: Body Language and Body Control

The story about facial coding is found in *The New York Times*, December 26, 2014, B-10; accessed online at http://www.nytimes.com/interactive/2014/12/26/sports/NBA-faces-data.html.

The research about lights on a screen can be found in Lior Suchard, *Mind Reader: Unlocking the Power of Your Mind to Get What You Want* (New York: William Morrow, 2012), 83.

The research about how body posture, facial expression, and general demeanor reveal our mood and how we are thinking is conveyed in Julius Fast, *Body Language* (New York: M. Evans & Company; rev. ed., 2002), 144.

W. K. Stratton describes in depth the three bouts between Patterson and Ingemar Johansson. See *Floyd Patterson: The Fighting Life of Boxing's Invisible Champion* (Boston & New York: Houghton Mifflin Harcourt, 2012), 94–135).

## Chapter 5: Work Ethic

Coach Percy Wells Cerutty's philosophy and technique are described in his book *Running with Cerutty*, a compendium of his writings for *Track & Field News*. This specific piece of advice is from the essay "What It Takes to Be a Champion" (Los Altos, CA: 1959), 1. This short book/pamphlet is a classic. Cerutty's running philosophy is clearly expressed in capsule form.

Olivia Prokopova's story is detailed in Sarah Lyall, "Mini-Golf as a Career? She Gets Past the Obstacles," *New York Times*, 15 August 2014, http://www.nytimes.com/2014/08/15/sports/golf/mini-golfs-fresh-face-not-a-clowns-olivia-prokopova.html?_r=0. In 2013, Prokopova became the first miniature golfer to ever win the triple crown of Mini Golf, which in her sport is the United States Open, the Master's, and the world championships.

Training and discipline are discussed in Brian Tracy, *No Excuses! The Power of Self-Discipline* (New York: Vanguard Press, 2010), 8, 17. Russell Sullivan in his book entitled *Rocky Marciano: The Rock of His Times* (Chicago: University of Illinois Press, 2002) grips the reader with interest from beginning to end. For example, what could have been boring about Marciano's early life comes to life with vivid and unforgettable images. The same is true of Marciano's fortunate encounter with his trainer and manager (45).

Canadian rower Adam Kreek is quoted in Jim Afremow, *The Champion's Mind: How Great Athletes Think, Train, and Thrive* (Emmaus, PA: Rodale, 2013), 191. As regards Michael Johnson and Alexander Popov see *Michael Johnson: Slaying the Dragon* (New York City: Regan Books, 1996) and PBS Home Video (*Atlanta's Olympic Glory: A Documentary* by Bud Greenspan, 1996).

Dan Gable details his philosophy in *A Wrestling Life: The Inspiring Stories of Dan Gable* (Bloomington: Indiana University Press, 2015), and in the especially inspiring book *Coaching Wrestling Successfully* (Champaign, IL: Human Kinetics, 1999.

David Blatt explains his childhood, career decisions, and training methods in Jack Maccallum, "Meet new Cleveland Cavaliers coach David Blatt: The King of Roam," *Sports Illustrated,* 11 August 2014, http://www.si.com/nba/2014/08/06/david-blatt-lebron-james-cleveland-cavaliers.

# Chapter 6: Goal Setting and Creating a Workout Blueprint

The SMART technique was devised by Gary Mack and is explained in his book *Mind Gym: An Athlete's Guide to Inner Excellence* (New York: McGraw Hill, 2001), 62.

In Arthur Lydiard's exercise plan from *Running to the Top* (89–117), one can find excellent training particulars for running events from 800 meters to the marathon.

For more on CrossFit, see Carl Paoli and Anthony Sherbondy, *Free+Style: Maximize Sport and Life Performance with Four Basic Movements* (New York City: Victory Belt Publishing, 2014), 9. Clayton Kershaw's story is told in Lee Jenkins, "It's on for L.A.'s Clayton Kershaw and Anze Kopitar," *Sports Illustrated* 30 September 2014, 36; http://www.si.com/vault/2014/10/06/106644058/the-real-ideal.

# Chapter 7: Preparing for the Workout

Tyler Varga's story is detailed in Zach Schonbrun, "Yale Running Back Confounds Opponents (and His Teammates, Too)," *New York Times,* 24 October 2014, http://www.nytimes.com/2014/10/25/sports/ncaafootball/tyler-varga-of-yale-blasts-off-to-an-unstoppable start.html?_r=0. If anyone is interested in finding the epitome of self-discipline, it is Tyler Varga.

Ellington Darden addresses the consequences of too little sleep in *The New High Intensity Training: The Best Muscle-Building System You've Never Tried* (New York: Rodale Books, 2004), 95.

The 2015 study from the journal *Sleep* was summarized by NPR as follows: "The adults who averaged five or six hours nightly during the study were four times more likely to catch the cold than people who slept at least seven hours per night. Analyzed another way: About 39 percent of those who slept six hours or less got sick. Of those who slept more than six hours, 'only 18 percent got colds,' Prather says. 'It's striking.'" Allison Aubrey, "Sleep More, Sneeze Less: Increased Slumber Helps to Prevent Colds," National Public Radio, 1 September 2015, http://www.npr.org/sections/health-shots/2015/09/01/436385137/aim-for-at-least-7-hours-of-sleep-nightly-to-fend-off-a-cold.

Stanford's research on why athletes require even more sleep than average teens and adults is discussed in Elizabeth Quinn, "Do Athletes Need Extra Sleep?", about.com, 16 December 2014, http://sportsmedicine.about.com/od/anatomyandphysiology/a/Athletes-Sleep.htm.

You can read about the positive impact of beet juice in your diet in William Imbo, "Can Beet Juice Help Your Athletic Performance?", *The Box*, 29 December 2014, http://boxlifemagazine.com/training/can-beet-juice-help-your-athletic-performance.

Echocardiograms are discussed in Peter Vigneron, "Inside the Debate on Athlete Heart Screenings," *Outside* magazine, December 2014, http://www.outsideonline.com/1928286/inside-debate-athlete-heart-screenings. While echocardiograms have saved the lives of a number of young athletes, they are not considered standard medical protocol for most people. See http://www.choosingwisely.org/societies/american-college-of-cardiology/ for the most recent recommendations of the American College of Cardiology.

## Chapter 8: Warming Up and Improving Flexibility

The classic book on how to stretch before a workout is Robert A. Anderson's *Stretching*, with detailed step-by-step illustrations by Jean Anderson. Three and a half million copies have been sold since it was released in 1980. See Robert A. Anderson, *Stretching: Thirtieth Anniversary Edition* (Bolinas, CA: Shelter Publications, 2010). You can access short videos based on the book at YouTube, including https://www.youtube.com/watch?v=3GOvf8rvpIc.

The benefits and hazards of yoga are explored in William J. Broad, *The Science of Yoga: The Risks and the Rewards* (New York: Simon & Schuster, 2012).

## Chapter 9: Strengthening the Core and Preventing Injury

The NIH research on core strength preventing "lower extremity" injury is found in Kellie C. Huxel Bliven and Barton E. Anderson, "Core Stability Training for Injury Prevention," *Sports Health* 5 (November 2013), available at http://www.ncbi.nlm. nih.gov/pmc/articles/PMC3806175/. The story about runners using core training to recover from injury is in "Why Traditional Sit-Ups and Ab Workouts Won't Help You Avoid Injury or Run Faster," *Runners Connect*, http://runnersconnect.net/running-injury-prevention/how-to-strengthen-your-core-for-running/.

Martin Rooney's exercises are found in *Warrior Cardio: The Revolutionary Metabolic Training System for Burning Fat, Building Muscle, and Getting Fit* (New York: William Morrow, 2012). A football star's functional fitness training regimen is described in Austin Murphy, "Pain Staking: An Exclusive Look at Drew Brees' Offseason Training," *Sports Illustrated* 30 July 2014, http://www.si.com/edge/2014/07/30/nfl-training-camp-saints-drew-brees.

For the fable of the Reed, see Marianne Moore's *The Fables of La Fontaine: A Complete Translation* (New York: Viking Adult, 1954), 33–34.

On HITT, or high-intensity interval training, see Jane E. Brody, "Sweaty Answer for Chronic Ills" *New York Times*, January 27, 2015, D-5; online as "Why Your Workout Should Be High-Intensity," http://well.blogs.nytimes.com/2015/01/26/sweaty-answer-to-chronic-illness/?_r=0.

Jordan Burroughs's words of inspiration can be found on his personal blog post, "Injuries Suck. Or Do They?" 9 November 2012, http://www.jordanburroughs.com/blog/injuries-suck-or-do-they-part-1.

## Chapter 10: Nutrition Matters: Top Four Super Foods for Peak Performance

For information on the Mediterranean Diet, see *The World's Healthiest Foods* (Seattle, WA: GMF Publishing, 2007) by George Mateljan, especially pages 37, 72, and 327.

For a guide that incorporates the Mediterranean Diet's principles in planning delicious, yet healthy meals, consult Donald D. Hensrud, Jennifer Nelson, Cheryl Forberg, Maureen Callahan, and Sheri Giblin, *The New Mayo Clinic Cookbook: Eating Well for Better Health* (Birmingham, AL: Oxmoor House, 2004).

For more on the excellent properties of nuts, see Joseph M. Kadans, *Encyclopedia of Fruits, Vegetables, Nuts and Seeds for Healthy Living* (West Nyack, NY: Parker Publishing Company, Inc., 1973), 66.

Guidelines about egg yolk consumption can be found in Kim McDevitt, "Eggs Should Be Part of Your Running Diet: Cracking the Truth," *Runner's World*, March 2015, 35; http://www.runnersworld.com/zelle-nutrition/eggs-should-be-a-part-of-your-running-diet.

Overhydration is addressed in Gretchen Reynolds, "For Athletes, the Risk of Too Much Water," *New York Times*, August 26, 2015, http://well.blogs.nytimes.com/2015/08/26/for-athletes-the-risk-of-too-much-water/?_r=0.

## Chapter 11: Never Give in to Adversity, but Know When a Change of Goal is in Your Interest

For the full story of Dallas Seavey's Iditarod win, see Dave Costello, "For This Man, the Iditarod Is a Father-Son Rivalry," *Outside*, February 12 2015, http://www.outsideonline.com/1931051/man-iditarod-father-son-rivalry. Seavey's time was eight days, thirteen hours, four minutes, and nineteen seconds. He has gone on to win the 2015 Iditarod.

## Chapter 12: The Psychology of Self-Discipline

Bernard Hopkins is profiled by Carlo Rotella in "Bernard Hopkins is Boxing's Oldest—and Most Cunning—Champion," *New York Times Magazine* (2 November

2014), http://www.nytimes.com/2014/11/02/magazine/bernard-hopkins-boxings-oldest-and-most-cunning-champion.html?_r=0.

Webster's Third New International Dictionary (2002) defines self-discipline as "the correction or regulation of oneself for the sake of improvement."

See Tom Verducci, "2014 Sportsman of the Year: Madison Bumgarner," Sports Illustrated (15 December 2014), http://www.si.com/sportsman/2014/12/09/madison-bumgarner-sports-illustrated-sportsman-profile.

## Chapter 13: Dealing with Failure

Meredith Kessler spoke of dealing with failure in a Triathlon magazine Special Issue (October 2014): http://triathlon.competitior.com/2014/09/photos/sneak-peek-triathlete-magazines-October-2014-issue_105236. Les Stroud's survival advice is given in "Would You Be Prepared for the End of Life as We Know It?" in Newsweek, March 7 2015, http://www.newsweek.com/would-you-be-prepared-end-life-we-know-it-311453.

You can read more about Yannick Agnel's outstanding attitude in Angelique Chrisafis, "France Hails Yannick Agnel, Its First Olympic Swimming Superstar," The Guardian, July 31 2012, http://www.theguardian.com/sport/2012/jul/31/france-olympic-swimming-yannick-agnel.

Renzo Gracie's technique for learning from failure is discussed in Sam Sheridan, The Fighter's Mind: Inside the Mental Game (New York: Grove Press, 2010), 235.

## Chapter 14: Dealing with Success

For a discussion of Tiger Wood's public scandals, see Lawrence J. Londino, Tiger Woods: A Biography (Westport, Connecticut: Greenwood Publishing Group, 2006).

## Chapter 15: Relationships and Personal Conduct

The Joshua Loth Liebman quote about kindness is found in his book Peace of Mind (New York: Simon and Schuster, 1966), 54.

Research on college athletes and mental wellness is found in Ann Kearns

Davoren and Seunghyun Hwang, "Mind, Body and Sport: Depression and Anxiety Prevalence in Student-athletes," October 8, 2014, http://www.ncaa.org/health-and-safety/sport-science-institute/mind-body-and-sport-depression-and-anxiety-prevalence-student-athletes.

Ted Johnson's story of brain injury is given in Michael Sweeney, *Brain: The Complete Mind* (Washington, D.C.: National Geographic Books, 2014), 160–61. Christina Kim's struggles with suicidal depression are reported in Karen Crouse, "Christina Kim Handles Downs and Ups by Dealing Openly with Depression," *New York Times*, 20 November 2014, http://www.nytimes.com/2014/11/21/sports/golf/christina-kim-feeling-better-after-battling-depression-is-revving-up-at-lpga-tour-championship.html?_r=0.

The Sayerville, New Jersey example was covered on 3 October 2014 in the Waco *Tribune Herald*, 3C. The University of Texas example is found in Patrick Tolbert, "UT Center for Sports Leadership and Innovation to Guide Young Athletes," 15 December 2014, http://kxan.com/2014/12/15/texas-to-set-up-program-to-guide-young-athletes/.

John McClaskey and Julian Bailes discuss performance-enhancing drugs in *When Winning Costs Too Much: Steroids, Supplements and Scandal in Today's Sports* (Lanhan, Maryland: Taylor Trade Publishing, 2006), 37, 105, 86. The use and consequences of these drugs are explored in Brian Chichester and Jack Croft, *Powerfully Fit: Dozens of Ways to Boost Strength, Increase Endurance, and Chisel Your Body*, Men's Health Life Improvement Guides series (Emmaus, Pennsylvania: Rodale Press, 1996), 131.

For more information on women's use of performance-enhancing drugs, see Dave Scheiber, "Female Athletes Are Not Immune to the Lures of Performance-Enhancing Drugs, *Tampa Bay Times*, April 5, 2008, http://www.tampabay.com/sports/basketball/college/female-athletes-are-not-immune-to-lure-of-performance-enhancing-drugs/444534.

## Chapter 16: Becoming a Team Leader

Marcus Aurelius's words are found in *Essential Works of Stoicism*, (New York City: Bantam Matrix Edition, 1965), 111.

Antonio Pierce's attitude toward cleanliness is profiled in Billy Witz, "Giants' Former Pro Bowler Leads a High School Powerhouse," a long feature article in the

*New York Times*, 26 September 2014, http://www.nytimes.com/2014/09/27/sports/football/ny-giants-former-pro-bowler-leads-a-high-school-powerhouse.html?_r=0.

## Chapter 17: Being Coachable

For research on the top reasons for job failure, see "Hiring for Attitude: Why 81% of New Hires Will Fail," Recruiting Division, April 23, 2014, http://www.recruitingdivision.com/why-new-hires-fail/.

August Turak's traits of coachable people are found in "Are You Coachable? The Five Steps to Coachability," *Forbes*, September 30, 2011, http://www.forbes.com/sites/augustturak/2011/09/30/are-you-coachable-the-five-steps-to-coachability/2/#7b898cfca83c.

## Chapter 18: Developing Your Mind and Preparing for the Future

For interesting infographics about the importance of communication skills in the workplace, see http://www.prdaily.com/Main/Articles/Listening_facts_you_never_knew_14645.aspx.

A Gallup poll discovered that the fear of public speaking affects 40 percent of American adults, making it the second-most-common fear after snakes (51 percent). See Geoffrey Brewer, "Snakes Top List of Americans' Fears," March 19, 2001, http://www.gallup.com/poll/1891/snakes-top-list-americans-fears.aspx.

Statistics from the National Institute for Literacy are discussed in "Reading and Literary Statistics," Raising Bookworms, http://raisingbookworms.com/resources/reading-and-literacy-statistics/, no date. CNN's research into the reading abilities of college athletes is found in Sara Ganim, "CNN Analysis: Some College Athletes Play Like Adults, Read Like Fifth-Graders," cnn.com, 8 January 2014, http://www.cnn.com/2014/01/07/us/ncaa-athletes-reading-scores/.

An excellent introduction to literature is Louis L'Amour's *Education of a Wandering Man* (New York: Bantam, 1990). Also recommended: Mortimer J. Adler's *How to Read a Book: The Classic Guide to Intelligent Reading* (New York: Simon and Schuster, 1940); Norman Lewis and Wilfred J. Funk, *30 Days to a More Powerful Vocabulary* (New York: Pocket Books, 1942); and Norman Lewis, *Word Power*

*Made Easy: The Complete Handbook for Building a Superior Vocabulary,* revised and expanded edition (New York: Anchor, 2014).

## Chapter 19: Coaching for Victory, Coaching for Life

The story about Kansas State's football coach, Bill Snyder, is from David Skretta, "K-State's Snyder Still Penning Old-school Notes," the Associated Press, 26 December 2014, http://collegefootball.ap.org/article/k-states-snyder-still-penning-old-school-notes.

Swim coach Kim Brackin outlined the way Millennials best learn how to improve in their sport in "How to Coach and Be Coached," *Austin Fit* Magazine, February 2015, http://www.austinfitmagazine.com/February-2015/How-to-Coach-and-Be-Coached/.

According to a 2014 *New York Times* article, Caldwell's first speech to the assembled players stressed their character rather than mentioning their reputation as bad boys: "He told them that by playing in a respectful way, they would get the respect they craved." Ben Spigel, "Thanks to a Cerebral Influence, the Lions Find Enlightenment: Detroit Lions Coach Jim Caldwell Finds Success with a Different Approach," *New York Times*, 21 December 2014, http://www.nytimes.com/2014/12/21/sports/football/detroit-lions-coach-jim-caldwell-finds-success-with-a-different-approach.html?_r=0.